REGINA'S CLOSET

Regina Reinharz Klein

REGINA'S CLOSET

Finding My Grandmother's Secret Journal

DIANA M. RAAB

BEAUFORT BOOKS
NEW YORK

Map on page iv from:
http://www.polishroots.com/genpoland/gal.htm

Library of Congress Cataloging-in-Publication Data

Raab, Diana, 1954–
Regina's closet : finding my grandmother's secret journal /
by Diana M. Raab.
p. cm.
Includes bibliographical references.
ISBN 978-0-8253-0575-7 (alk. paper)
1. Klein, Regina Reinharz, 1903–1964 — Childhood and youth.
2. World War, 1914–1918 — Children — Poland. 3. World War,
1914–1918 — Personal narratives, Polish. 4. World War, 1914–1918 —
Jews — Poland — Biography. 5. Orphans — Austria — Biography.
6. Polish Americans — Biography. I. Title.

D639.C4R27 2007
940.3'161092 — dc22
[B]
2007018161

Published in the United States by Beaufort Books, New York
www.beaufortbooks.com
Distributed by Midpoint Trade Books, New York
www.midpointtradebooks.com

8 6 4 2 10 9 7 5 3 1

PRINTED IN THE UNITED STATES OF AMERICA

This book is dedicated to Regina Reinharz Klein,
whose life ended too soon.

June 22, 1903–September 7, 1964

KINGDOM OF POLAND

Tarnobrzeg
Mielec
Lubaczów
Rzeszów Jarosław
Kraków
Oświęcim Tarnów Jasło
Bochnia
Biała Myślenice Nowy Sącz Krosno Sanok
Nowy Targ
Orava
Spis

Rawa
Przemyśl
Ustrzyki Drohobycz

Sambor
Sambir

RUSSIAN EMPIRE

Bełz
Brody
Busk
Złoczów
Zolochiv

Lviv
Lwów

Zbaraż

Brzeżany
Berezhany Tarnopol
Ternopil

Stryj Bohatyn
Kałusz Halicz Czortków Husiatyn
Chortkiv

Bolechów
Bolekhiv Stanisławów Zaleszczyki
Ivanofrankivsk

AUSTRIAN EMPIRE

Kołomyja

Galicia, before World War I

We are, all of us, molded and remolded by those who have loved us, and though that love may pass, we remain nonetheless their work — a work that very likely they do not recognize and which is never exactly what they intended.

— François Mauriac, *The Desert of Love*

Contents

PART THREE

A Note to the Reader

This book is based on the retrospective journal my grand-mother wrote in English in the late 1930s after her arrival in the United States. The journal begins with her child-hood during World War I and ends with her immigration to the United States.

The book contains details gathered from interviews with my mother, my grandmother's niece, Derora, her cousins, and her brother-in-law, Igo. The book also in-cludes information gathered from various other refer-ences and historical documents relating to certain events and locales, all of which provided a complete picture of her time and place. In addition, the book has some of my own insights into my grandmother's life and some projec-tion onto her past.

Writing this book was my way to re-examine my grandmother's life, now more than forty years after her death. My intention was to understand her life and what might have caused her to end it in such a tragic way. The project has also helped to heal the wounds caused by los-ing her at such a young age.

Regina and Diana, 1957

Acknowledgments

To my husband, Simon Raab, for everything.

To Eva Marquise, my mother, for passing on my grandmother's journal and without whom this project would not have been possible.

To my mentors and friends at Spalding University: Connie May Fowler, Richard Goodman, Luke Wallin, Ellie Bryant, Roy Hoffman, Charles Gaines, Jeannie Thompson, Dianne Aprille, Sena Jeter Naslund, and Karen Mann for their encouragement and support.

To my earliest readers and reviewers: Beatrice Bowles, Kim Crum, Philip F. Deaver, Cheryl Dellasega, Tish Dowd, Julie Dunsworth, George Getshow, Alice Gorman, Lois Gilbert, Kaylene Johnson, Judy Kellum, Loren London, Mimi London, Jed Marquisee, Victoria Moon, Joan and Frank Pohl, Mary Popham, Susan Treitz, and Pamela White.

To Gail Kearns for her ongoing support and enthusiasm for this project and who provided the historical backdrop painting the landscape of my grandmother's era.

To Carol del Vitto and Gisela Cartmill for translating some of my grandmother's original documents and readings from German to English.

To Maggie Lang for her positive energy and relentless technical support.

To my publisher, David Nelson, and editor, Margot Atwell, for believing in this project from the beginning.

To family and friends who shared what they remembered about my grandmother: Igo Klein (her brother-in-law), Bob and Silva Marquisee, Maddy Robbins (her doctor's wife), Faith Stern (her cousin), Derora Reinharz (her niece), and my cousin David Nameri .

Others for their inspiration, encouragement and curiosity during the various stages of this project: Alex and Jeannine Raab, Lilly Berenhaut, Norma Dvorsky, Serena and Frank Goitanich, Kim and David Raab, Nancy and Andre Raab, Jack and Agi Mandel, Ivan and Genevieve Reitman, Elliott Figman, Jennifer Benka, Cheryl Klein, Darlyn Finch, Susan Gulbransen, Jean Harfenist, Steve Beisner, Melinda Palacio, Susan Pitcher, and Susan Chiavelli.

Conversations with Kelly Cherry, Eva Hoffman, Phillip Lopate, Honor Moore, Rachel Simon, and Tobias Wolff.

To my children, Rachel Miriam, Regine Anna, and Joshua Samuel, for their love and support during the writing process and who understood when the muse was at work and waved without entering my writing studio.

To my beloved father, Edward Marquise, (1921–1991) who my grandmother absolutely adored.

PART ONE

CHAPTER 1

Grandma Takes Her Life

September 1964

I was ten years old the morning I found my grandmother dead. Our neighborhood in Queens was serene while many residents were out of town celebrating the last three-day weekend of the summer. My mother and father weren't at home, and my grandfather was visiting his sister Rusza in Paris.

I knocked on Grandma's bedroom door. She didn't answer. I cracked the door open and got a whiff of her perfume, Soir de Paris (Evening in Paris). Out of the corner of my eye, I spotted the sheer white curtains swaying in front of the open window overlooking the street. The air in her room was crisp, and the night's dampness clung to the wooden floor. Grandma's bed, one of two single beds pushed close together, was beside the window.

Grandma lay beneath her soft, checkered Scandinavian wool blanket with fringed edges. She called it the warmest blanket in the world. On her headboard rested a

Graham Greene novel *The End of the Affair,* a hairbrush, a box of Kleenex, and an open bottle of prescription pills.

"Grandma," I called softly from the doorway, "can I go to Cindy's?"

She didn't answer. I glanced at my new watch. It was already ten o'clock in the morning. On most days Grandma was the first one into the maroon and pink-tiled bathroom that all five of us shared. I walked inside to see if her toothbrush was wet. It was still dry from the night before, but her towel, slung sideways on the towel rack was damp. The toilet cover was down, just the way she taught me to leave it. I didn't remember hearing the sound of running water that morning, a sound often heard within the walls of our older house.

In my fluffy blue slippers, I returned to Grandma's room and tiptoed around Grandpa's bed toward Grandma's side. I gently tapped her shoulder.

"Grandma," I repeated, "can I please go swimming at Cindy's? I'll be back by lunchtime. Promise." Still no answer. Grandma's face looked pale and her eyes were loosely shut, as if she were almost ready to get up.

I sensed something was seriously wrong. I tiptoed out of the room, glancing over my shoulder in the hope that she'd wake up and answer me. Under the weight of my footsteps, the wooden floor made cracking sounds. Grandma's closet door was closed and her makeup was spread out on her vanity. I trembled while scurrying toward my parents' room at the end of the hallway. They also had two single beds pushed together with one headboard and two pale pink electric blankets sprawled out on each bed. The beds were unmade, and on my father's bedside table was an empty plate with crumbs left from a sandwich he had eaten the night before. The oblong wooden bedside table had a glass covering it with a display of family photographs beneath. One photo caught my eye. My grandmother was leaning against a tree in our backyard. She had a broad smile and seemed playful, the way I will always remember her.

I looked at the pink dial phone, but was afraid to pick it up. I glanced at the phone book beside it, which had my mother's horse stable's phone number inside. My mother was careless about many things, but not her telephone book. She had every number imaginable in that book, and when it became illegible, she splurged on a new one and copied all the numbers over. I dialed the stable. That day she'd be riding in the ring, and not in the woods, so the stable boy would certainly pick up the phone. Frantically, I asked to speak to my mother.

"Mom, I think something's wrong with Grandma," I blurted quickly. "She's not answering when I talk to her."

"What?" My mother said so loudly I had to hold the phone away from my ear.

"Mom. Come home. I'm scared," I said, bending my knees up and down as if I had to go to the bathroom, even though I had just been.

"I'm on my way." My mother hung up before I could take my next breath.

For a few moments I stood staring at the phone, and then picked it up again to call my father at work, but he was out of the store on his coffee break. I needed to talk to someone. I was petrified. I wondered what to do. I was afraid to go back into my grandmother's room. Should I wait in the living room, or the front lawn, or at Grandma's side? If she had awakened, she would have called me. Finally, I ran downstairs and then ran right back up again, feeling lost in my own home. I ran into my room and grabbed the Tiny Tears doll off my bed and then dashed back downstairs, slipping in haste down the last two steps.

I waited near the living room window, walking in circles like a cat chasing its tail. I hugged Tiny Tears so tightly that she wet her pants. The water I had poured into the hole in her back to make her tears must have leaked out. I didn't want to go back upstairs for another diaper. I was too scared.

I finally settled on the bay window near the front door. I sat cuddled up on the ledge as I had so many times before, waiting for my parents to drive in at the end of the day. My nose was glued to the cool glass. This time more than ever, I was anxious for an adult to pull up.

Soon an ambulance siren stirred the ordinarily quiet residential neighborhood, and the vehicle pulled up in front of our house facing the wrong way, against traffic. From the other direction came another set of flashing lights and the siren of a police car. The policeman flung his car door open toward the curb and dashed up to the house. Terror grabbed me amidst all the commotion. Three firemen followed the policeman, and before I knew it, strangers were invading our home. My mother came home from the stable, and my father returned from work in his pink Chevrolet, the one that matched the house. They parked one behind the other in the driveway.

Uniformed paramedics, their blue short-sleeved shirts rolled up to reveal bulging muscles, made their way up the four stairs to our front door. They passed the Japanese cherry tree that my parents had planted on the front lawn the year I was born. It wasn't in bloom, and its bare branches echoed the coldness I felt inside. The paramedics brushed by the dying rhododendron bushes on either side of the steps and flung open the screen door. They asked flatly where my grandmother was, charging past me as if I were part of the décor. I felt like a stranger in my own home.

"Just stay right there," said one, as I started to climb the stairwell to see Grandma.

Standing at the bottom of the stairs looking up, I fiddled with my clammy hands and crossed my legs, afraid to run to the bathroom because I might miss something. What were they doing to my beloved grandmother? Were they lifting her up, trying to get her to walk? My mother came in, kissed my forehead, and then took off after the paramedics. The fragrance of her perfume seemed to linger longer than usual. My father, who tended to become queasy in medical situations, stood outside the house speaking with the ambulance driver, looking ashen and nervous while he paced from the house to the street. He must have been too nervous to light up a cigarette, something he would often do when he was under stress.

My eyes remained fixed on the mirror on the linen closet door at the top of the stairs. They would have to pass it before bringing Grandma down. The year before, I had seen ghosts in that mirror. It was the night I drank Coke at bedtime. I woke up in the middle of the night and on the way to the bathroom, passed by the mirror, where I saw something that spooked me, and so I scooted back to bed. After that night, I always made sure my parents left the hall light on. I never wanted to see those ghosts again.

Soon I spotted two paramedics grasping both ends of the stretcher my grandmother was strapped to. With quick and urgent steps, they transported her down the steep stairs leading to the front door. I wondered what would happen if they slipped and Grandma went flying.

As the stretcher approached the bottom of the stairs where I was still standing, I noticed my grandmother's stiffness and how her eyes were tightly shut. I inched close to her and whispered, "Grandma," my last hope of ever hearing her voice. I felt the paramedic's eyes on mine, as he tossed me a sympathetic glance.

My mother followed behind and gave me a rushed hug.

"You stay home with Daddy," she said. "That'll be the best."

"Will Grandma be okay?" I asked, looking for solace in her dark brown eyes, but finding none.

Soon after my grandmother died, my parents had a barbeque with some friends and family. In the corner of our backyard I saw my mother talking with a couple of her friends. They were whispering, so it must have been important. I stood by the backyard window straining to hear what they were saying. It was then that I heard my mother tell her friends that my grandmother had killed herself by taking too many sleeping pills.

Because I was the only one home with my grandmother the day she died, I felt responsible for her death, but my mother assured me that it wasn't my fault and my grandmother's death had nothing to do with anything I had done. I really wanted to believe her.

Regina, 1964

Diana 1964, the year Regina died

CHAPTER 2

A Journal Discovered

May 1997

A few months short of my forty-third birthday, my mother came for a weekend visit to our home just north of Orlando, Florida. In those days, we were permitted to greet passengers at their arrival gate at the airport, so my son Josh and I stood at the end of the gate's ramp. Josh, eight years old at the time, proudly held a bouquet of flowers for his grandmother. In the best of times, my mother was a slow walker and only traveled with one carry-on bag. Her hips were uneven, as a result of a horseback-riding accident thirty years earlier, making her wobble when she walked and obviously more recognizable in a crowd.

One thing my mother always stuck into her suitcase when she flew in from New York was some sort of nostalgic item from either my father or from one of my grandparents. You could say that my mother lived in the past, and this was one of the ways this became evident to me.

My father died in 1991 from congestive heart failure,

probably secondary to forty years of smoking. A few times each year my parents would take the seven-hour drive to visit, but now my mother flew by herself.

At dinnertime on the night of her arrival, my husband, Simon, and I were busy darting around, tidying up, and making dinner while our three kids — ages eight, twelve, and fourteen years old — played in the family room. My mother peeked in on them and then walked back to the kitchen. She lifted her suitcase onto one of the six contemporary black leather chairs at the table.

She pulled something out and yelled to no one in particular, "This is for you." She had done this many times before, sometimes going as far as plunking the item on the kitchen table, only to mention it later in passing. But this time it was different.

"This is your grandmother's," she continued, as I stood at the counter, my back to her with my hands submerged in a bowl of chopped meat. I suspected she was speaking to me, so I turned around as she flung a plastic sheath filled with papers across my glass kitchen table.

"I'll leave it here," she said, as if it were the daily newspaper, something to be read with an afternoon cup of coffee. My mother was rarely tactful, so this maneuver didn't particularly stun me. Curious nevertheless, I went to the sink, washed my hands, grabbed the sheath off the table, and followed her into the family room.

What she had tossed me were the pages of my grandmother's journal. It wasn't a bound book or a notebook, but was a transparent sheath filled with about fifty pages of single-spaced typed pages, laden with strikeovers, awkward syntax, and numerous grammatical errors. As I looked, a sudden surge of memories came from the day my grandmother taught me how to type on her Remington typewriter, which had been perched on the vanity in her room next to mine. I wondered if she used that Remington to type her journal.

"Have a seat," she had said, pointing me to her vanity chair.

"I'm going to teach you how to type. This is a handy skill for a girl to have, plus you never know what kind of stories you'll have to tell one day."

She stood behind me, smiling radiantly in the mirror. She took my right hand and positioned it on the second row from the bottom, carefully placing one finger on each letter. With my left hand, she repeated the same gesture.

"This is the position your fingers should be in. When you become a good typist, you won't even have to look at the letters while you're typing. Okay, dear, let's see if we can type your name."

With my left middle finger she had me press on the *D*. Then we moved to the right middle finger and moved up a row to type an *I*. Then my pinky pressed the *A*, and then something really tricky had to happen: I had to move my right index finger down to the bottom row to type an *N*. Then my left pinky typed an *A* again. After each letter I glanced up at the paper to see the impression my efforts were making. After reaching the last *A* in my name, I proudly looked up at my grandmother's face in the mirror.

"You see, you did it!" she said, squeezing my shoulders. "Like anything in life, the more you practice, the better you'll become. You must work hard to get results; you'll learn that soon enough, my love."

That typing lesson reflected the essence of the relationship between my beloved grandmother and me. She always advocated independence and my becoming a self-actualized person like herself.

❧

I carefully removed the journal pages from the sheath and noticed they were yellowing, fragile to touch, and some edges were slightly torn. I was scared to hold them and afraid to put them down — scared that all those cherished memories could get lost or ruined. What if someone spilled coffee on this journal?

"How long have you had this? How come you're so casual about giving it to me?" I asked my mother.

"I wasn't sure if you'd be interested."

"What? Are you crazy? How could I not be interested?"

"Well, then, I'm glad I stuck it in my suitcase. I found it when I was going through some papers in her closet," she said, sitting down on the sofa beside where my son was assembling a Lego house on the carpet.

"Did you read what she wrote?" I asked.

"No. I know what happened to her. Why should I have to read about it?" I stormed out holding the papers, passed the kitchen, and marched directly into my office. After closing the sliding wooden door, I kicked off my shoes and swung my legs onto the sofa. I adjusted the animal print pillow behind my head and opened to the first page.

It took only a few moments for me to be immersed in her story, mesmerized by her childhood pain and swept away by her sense of rhetoric. Her voice lifted off the page. I wanted to hug her and take her into my arms and soothe her. Yet, at the same time, her epic gave me strength and hope as to what a woman can endure and how someone can survive in spite of all odds. I thought about my own recent survival story and journey with breast cancer and felt I needed my grandmother's love more than ever. I felt our survival stories were a thread that bound us together.

I read each word, felt every intonation, each pain, and every rare moment of joy. It was impossible to stop reading. My eyes began burning from smudged mascara. I read the pages wanting to know everything about my grandmother and to infuse myself with her essence. A part of me hoped to capture some love from her story — love that I missed so much. Another part of me wanted to hear her speak about me. But, as it turned out, she had written this journal many years before my birth.

While reading, my grandmother's wonderful spirit reentered my life, and I loved that. For the first time since she died, I was reunited with her. The feeling was both eerie and exciting. Her voice once again filled the gap of my loneliness as an only child. It also served as a reminder of my sense of abandonment when she left me when I was ten.

Since that day, I have read and reread the journal. My intent has been to capture her sensibilities and understand who she was and what she had endured. Holding the pages of her journal grounded me with an intense amount of security and love.

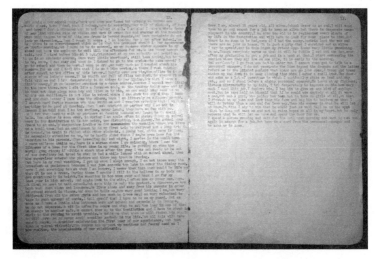

Regina's journal

PART TWO

CHAPTER 3

Born in Galicia

My grandmother Regina Reinharz Klein was born in Kalush, Galicia, on June 22, 1903. Galicia was the name given to the partition of Poland occupied by the Austro-Hungarian Empire between 1772 and 1918. Today the name Galicia has faded and no longer appears on the maps of the Polish Republic as a country, province, or region.

The town of Kalush is located in the western part of Ukraine at the foot of the Carpathian Mountains. The first written records of Kalush dates back to 1437. It started as a village that became a town in 1549 and was part of Austria-Hungary and Poland before being incorporated into the Soviet Union in 1939. The city received its independence when the Soviet Union collapsed in 1991. Today it is a sister city of Grand Prairie, Texas, and has a population of 73,500, almost entirely culturally Ukrainian except for a small Russian population.

Historically, from the sixteenth century, there had

been a strong Jewish presence in the city. According to the census of 1765, there were 1,087 Jews in Kalush who paid poll tax. They owned nearly 130 buildings in the city. The great synagogue was finished in 1825. Around 1880, 4,266 Jews lived in Kalush, and by 1910, there were 4,363 Jews, about half the total population. That number rose to 6,000 between the two world wars. In 1941, Kalush was "ethnically cleansed" by the Nazis.

My grandmother's journal begins during her childhood at age eleven during the outbreak of World War I as she describes her family environment and life on the streets of Kalush — the bloodshed, the horror, and the battles.

I am a war child, and here is my story. I was born an undesired child, a girl added to two brothers. When my mother [Ethel], after her delivery, was told I was a girl, she fainted. When she came to her senses, she said she would gladly kill me because of my being a girl. She said she would have preferred six boys to one female, because, she argued, a female suffers too much in this world. I grew up and quickly distinguished good from bad treatment. I saw that she discriminated against me and acted as if she resented my being born — as if it were my fault. I spent a lot of time on the streets. Everyone in the community really liked me. I was amiable and beguiling and always willing to help others.

A few times each week, I would open my bedroom window and climb out to the street below. I tried being as quiet as possible because my sister, who was four years younger, slept in the same room. But she never woke up. I would then wander up the street chatting with the Ukrainian peasants and watching as they brought cows, pigs, and eggs to the local market. It was here where I learned some basic entrepreneurial skills. Day after day I dealt with those "petty bargaining professional buyers."

Many of the buyers came from miles away. Even during the winter months, when there was sleet or snow, they wore very thin shoes because they could not afford the luxury of winter wear. Many arrived at the market tired, hungry, and eager to make a good deal. Those who had more money arrived at the market wearing leather shoes. They would step down onto the street from their self-built wooden wagons. The ends of the wagons had these wooden sticks resembling the tails of pigs. As soon as the wagons pulled up in town, me and other children from the village ran after them and jumped up on the sticks to get a free ride up the street. We hung onto the wagon for a while, well at least until the peasant turned around, slapped his whip, and yelled at us. This sent all of us scurrying into the nearby alleys.

Reading my grandmother's journal, I noticed how revealing she was about her mother neither wanting nor loving her. From an early age, my grandmother had an incredibly free spirit, and she exerted it whenever the opportunity presented itself. I'll never know if that spirit was a result of her not sensing motherly love or if it was simply a part of her inborn personality. I speculate that it was a combination of the two.

Because my grandmother didn't believe that her mother loved her, she sought attention and adoration from other adults. She reached out to those in her village by running errands and assisting them with their chores. Later on in her life, I believe that she transferred this need for attention and love to my mother and me. By giving herself completely, she received our love in return.

Like most children who did not receive unconditional motherly love, my grandmother was left with indelible scars. The fact that she recounted in her journal painful incidents from her childhood tells me that her mother's negative attitude had a huge impact on her.

One Saturday morning when I was about five years old, I woke up early and wanted to surprise my mother by washing all the windows in our small house, which sat in a row of houses along the street. There were many small panes of glass and I had to wash each one individually. It took me a long time, and maybe I rushed the job wanting to get it done before my mother woke up. After washing for about one hour, I accidentally broke a window and it shattered all over the kitchen floor. Thankfully, no one woke up to all the noise. I was devastated, because I knew that it didn't take much for my mother to be angry at me, and this would surely upset her. It's not that we didn't have the money for a new window; we did. It's just that she did not respond well to any change or mishap in her daily routine, plus she was very particular about her house, especially her kitchen.

I stood completely still, afraid to move. Suddenly, I heard my mother's bedroom door open and she staggered out half asleep. She came toward me standing still in the kitchen. I looked down and thank goodness I was wearing my slippers, which sometimes she accused me of not wearing. I didn't want her to be mad about two things. I was petrified at what she might say or do. She was so unpredictable. Instead of asking me what I was doing or even saying thank you for washing the windows, she yelled at me and asked how I could do such a thing. I was afraid to answer, because no matter what I said, she would still be angry. She began spanking me and then sent me off to my room.

I was really astonished to read this scene. I wondered how a mother could be so cruel to a well-meaning daughter. Although my grandmother didn't describe her mother's physical appearances, I imagined Ethel short in stature, about five feet tall, with her black hair pulled back tightly in a bun. I also imagined her as quite short-tempered, and the window incident, which had even further repercussions, was a perfect example of that.

My mother was so angry about this incident that on Monday morning she walked into my room, shook me, and told me to immediately come to the kitchen for breakfast. While gulping down my second bowl of warm semolina, my mother turned to me and said, "It's time that you begin school, Regina. You'll be less trouble if you're at school and away from this house. This will be the best thing for both of us." She told me to run off to my room and get dressed appropriately, because we would be leaving before the clock struck seven.

My mother then dragged me across the village and through the same marketplace where I had made local friends during my sojourns in our village. I did not go willingly to this school. I screamed and kicked as my mother grasped my wrist, dragging me through the early morning crowds. A few times I tried to break loose from her grip, but to no avail.

My mother's anger about the mishap was intractable. If she had her way, she would surely have had me tied up at school, never to see me again. When we arrived at the school, my mother approached the elderly janitor who was sweeping the floors. She asked for directions to the headmaster's office. My mother stormed inside the office, telling the headmaster that she wanted to register me in the school. On that day I was frugally dressed in a plaid dress covered with a white apron splattered with stains. My brown tie-up shoes were polished, but obviously old. My auburn hair was braided halfway down my back, and my brown eyes stared up at the mistress, who insisted that five years old was too young for a child to begin school. Like a specimen, she scanned me up and down and said, "Even if she is a mature little girl, she is still too young."

My mother looked deep into the headmaster's eyes, put her hands on her hips, and said that I was no good at home because all I did was break windows. She lied and said that I left the house every day through my bedroom window and not through the door.

I was unable to explain to the headmaster that I used the window to escape the threat of punishment. My mother didn't want me to wander the streets, but she gave me little choice. I just had to escape her anger. Finally, the headmaster agreed to admit me to the school.

I did not like that school and did not want to go, and so every day my mother had to drag me there. As we approached the long path leading to the front entrance, the other kids were greatly amused by my yelling, screaming, and crying. In the classroom, I was told to sit in the last row, where I couldn't see the blackboard through the heads of about forty children. The best thing was being away from my witch of a mother. In the privacy of the school environment, I could eat and play as I pleased. The only time the teacher became angry with me was when I spoke out of turn to my friends.

I was so happy six months later when we got our report cards. It made me feel so mature, like my older brothers, Willy and Herman. I ran home from school and handed my mother the envelope. I was thrilled to have all satisfactory grades, but I still detested attending that school.

By the end of the first term, winter arrived, and it took much longer to arrive at school. There was so much snow that our house was often covered up to the roof. Each day, before getting dressed, I pushed aside my curtains and glanced down at the street below. All I could see was the white ground cover. I could see neither a road nor a path. On those stormy days my father, Lieb, as he sometimes liked me calling him, walked me to school. He wore his long winter coat, making him appear even taller than his six-foot-tall frame. I felt so short beside him. His thick white hair hung over the collar of his winter coat. When he walked, he pushed the shovel in front of us to pave our way.

I cried the entire way to school, repeatedly telling my father how much I hated it there, and continued to plead with him to take me home. He stopped, turned around, and pulled a white handkerchief from his pocket to dry my tears.

"It'll be okay," he said, "you'll get used to it." I told him that I hated the school because the older teacher always embarrassed me and asked questions that were impossible to answer. When we finally arrived at school, my father gave me a big hug and kiss, as I continued to plead with him to take me back home.

One morning my father walked me into class and we noticed another teacher, a much younger one, standing before the blackboard. This new teacher announced that the older teacher was ill and would not be returning to school. As it turned out, I really liked this new teacher much better because she placed the smallest students on the benches in front of the class, instead of scattering them throughout the class. Since I was one of the smallest children, I was happy to be the first child in the first row.

In accordance with God's word, the smallest and poorest shall come nearest to him. After the first week, the new teacher sent a note home with all the children informing them that she was the new teacher. I ran home as fast as I could and handed it to my mother. I stood before her in the hallway patiently waiting for her to remove the note from the envelope. My mother's eyes scanned the note twice, from top to bottom, and then returned it to the envelope. Suddenly, she put on an angry expression. I was so scared of getting her mad, and didn't remember doing anything wrong at school. In a resentful tone, she told me that she was being called to school to meet the new teacher. I sighed with relief. The following day, I accompanied my mother to school for the meeting and hid behind the classroom door while the two of them spoke.

I expected to hear harsh words, because that's all I heard my mother say about me. I thought the teacher would do the same, but what I heard made me cry with joy, because the young teacher repeated over and over again, "She is a good child, she is a good child."

As it turned out, that teacher was the best addition to my young life.

She stood by me during the entire war. She told me that even though I was the smallest girl in the class, I was the smartest and best behaved. Summer vacation rolled around, and once again I became tortured by being around my mother all day long and being exposed to her belittling comments. I could never do right by her. I couldn't wait to go back to school. All summer long I lay on my checkered blanket writing unsent letters to my favorite teacher and praying that I would have her for the next grade.

The following year my grandmother wrote:

By the time I turned nine, I wondered if one of the reasons for my mother being nervous and short-tempered was because of my parents' faltering marriage. I was just not sure why my parents constantly bickered. Each evening after dinner, as they cleared the dishes, they found something to get angry and yell about. It was usually because of a silly and insignificant issue, such as why my father did not put the garbage out on time. The bickering would sometimes continue into the night and behind their bedroom door. These arguments left Beronia [her sister] and me with a sense of uneasiness, but finally we realized that there was little we could do to change things.

If the arguments happened during the day, my mother would sometimes retreat for quiet time to the outside porch. From her rocking chair she would stare blankly out at the main street of Kalush. Sometimes she distracted herself by mending our family's socks.

This entry in my grandmother's journal was an especially sad realization for me. Through the accounts of people, albeit scarce, who lived in Kalush during this period, I got a glimpse of daily life: how close and affectionate families were and how much the Jews loved their hometown. Unfortunately, my grandmother did not have this close-knit family situation in which to thrive.

In his essay, "Kalush: Our Native Town" from the Yizkor book *Kalush: The Life and Destruction of the Community,* Moyshe Ettinger writes,

> Kalush was built like most Galician towns which had their origins in the sixteenth and seventeenth centuries. Its hub or "ring" was the square marketplace. All around its four sides stood one- and two-story buildings, with shop fronts and cellars, the properties of the more prosperous householders. The "ring" was the trading center, from which radiated the streets and alleys of the town.

The marketplace he describes must have been the one frequented by my grandmother and the one where her mother pulled an unwilling Regina to school when she was five years old. All these readings have helped me visualize and understand the environment in which my beloved grandmother was raised, and have helped answer some questions I have had since her passing.

My grandmother shared this compelling scene:

On some days my mother was particularly lonely. There is one day in particular that I will never forget. It was the day my mother summoned us one at a time to join her on the porch.

My brother Willy, the eldest at nineteen, was called first, and he walked outside with both arms crossed, standing about four feet from our mother.

"Willy, I've been thinking about what you kids should be when you

grow up. You, my son, shall be a clerk. You're very good with handling money and finances. I think this type of work will bring you much happiness in your life. Now carry on and get your little sister and brother. I also have some news for them."

Willy walked back inside the house, and Herman, the next oldest in the family, who was seventeen, stepped onto the porch. He approached our mother and stood at the prescribed spot four feet away.

"Herman, you, my son, shall become some sort of merchant. You have a way with people and you're a good salesman. I remember when you were a little boy when we had a small store. You always asked to stand behind the counter selling. All the customers wanted to buy from you. You made the people laugh with your jokes. Yes. A merchant, that's what I see for you," she said.

Next, Beronia, the youngest at seven years of age, stepped outside.

"You, my daughter, I think the best thing for you is to be a housewife. You're so helpful in the kitchen and in tidying up the house. You will make someone a good wife one day, and surely a good mother. You have so much patience with those little dolls we bought you last year for your birthday."

Next, my mother asked me at the age of eleven to come out onto the porch.

"And you, Regina. What can I say about a girl who is so clumsy in the house, always breaking things? What kind of job will be awaiting you?"

I stood paralyzed waiting to hear my mother's next words.

Finally, she continued, *"It perhaps shall be a surprise to hear me say that you have the potential to go the farthest of your brothers and sister. You are such a clever child. You're always reading, always studying, and always with a book in your hand. The kitchen, my dear, is not for you. You're very good with people, and you need to get out into the world and do some good. For you, I think you should become a doctor. Just think how many people you could help."*

I remained completely still and then ran over to my mother and gave her a big hug. She held me only for only a brief moment before telling me that it didn't mean that I would be excused from household responsibilities. "Now run along," she said, "the table must be set for dinner, and the clothes need to be taken down from the clothing line."

Soon after that incident on the porch in June 1914 and just after my grandmother turned eleven, there were rumblings of the beginnings of World War I. My grandmother's father was one of the townspeople who represented the town's intelligentsia, and they were the first to sense the imminent war.

My grandmother wrote this of her father's political beliefs:

My father had strong beliefs in the Austro-Hungarian realm and felt that it was there to stay. "Woe to the foe of that crown," he told us when we asked if it was time to be concerned about an impending war. To secure our small amount of savings, my father invested in war loans. That was the first duty of every patriot. A few days later my father walked into the bank, and it was on that day when the first battalions of Hungarian hussars marched against the Russian enemies.

Within a week, the war broke out. Just like any other day, we woke up at the crack of dawn. My mother was preparing breakfast, and Beronia and I were rolling around in our beds, getting ready to throw our covers off and get ready for a new day of school. We got up to make our beds, and in the next room I heard my brothers bickering about who was to clean up the room that they shared. My father was already in the living room reading his morning paper. As he called us all to the living room to gather around, I heard my mother drop a dish in the kitchen. When we entered, my father tossed the newspaper on the coffee table.

*He abruptly stood up from the sofa, took a deep breath, and said,
"War has been declared, but don't worry. The Kaiser will easily win."*

At the time, many people shared my great-grandfather's sentiment. In 1914 no one expected the war would last four years and cost more than 9 million lives. A majority of nationalities in the Austro-Hungarian Empire, including the Jews, wholeheartedly supported the war. It was the perfect chance to demonstrate their loyalty to the Hapsburg dynasty and to the Austro-Hungarian state.

The chaos during June and July of that year was unbelievable. In July 1914, Kaiser Wilheim II was asked to return home early from his vacation. Even before coming home, the German government had already rejected Serbia's request for mediation. In essence, the war was caused by the struggle to restore the balance of European power after the emergence of Germany as a nation.

There was another prevailing reason for Jewish support for the war. Bruce Pauley writes about it in his book *From Prejudice to Persecution: A History of Austrian Anti-Semitism.*

For them [the Jews] Russia, home to more than half of the world's Jewish population and by far the worst and most powerful oppressor of their coreligionists, was the instigator of the war and the monarchy's principal enemy. Jewish newspapers even held the Russian government responsible for the murder of Franz Ferdinand in Sarajevo. Princip, the assassin, and the Serbian government were no more than tools of the

Russians. When the Russian "steamroller" swept through most of Galicia in 1914, it was interpreted not so much as a defeat for Austria-Hungary as it was proof of Russia's preparedness for an invasion.

My history classes taught me that the war was triggered by the assassination in Serbia of Franz Ferdinand, the archduke of Austria-Hungary, which then declared war on Serbia. The Russians were bound by treaty to Serbia, and that's why they mobilized their army. Germany then declared war on Russia. France then declared war on Germany and therefore on Austria-Hungary.

Because my entire family comes from Europe, the war touched all of my roots. My grandfather was born in Poland, my mother was born in Austria, and my father was born in Germany.

I was so deeply affected by this early section of my grandmother's journal that, after reading it, I sat paralyzed in the armchair in my study. I felt honored to have received such a treasure from my grandmother — a document that so eloquently painted the landscape of her childhood and helped me understand my own roots.

At the same time, I was struck by a deeper sense of kinship with my grandmother because of our love for writing, our nurturing ways, and how our mothers had such similar characteristics. Obviously, our mothers loved us, but they both seemed to have this inability to display their love toward us. They also had a knack for making us feel insecure about ourselves. To compensate for this missing link in our lives, my grandmother and I sought approval from others, such as neighbors and teachers.

∞

My grandmother's story about breaking her mother's window triggered a memory from my own childhood. For my twelfth birthday, my mother passed on a family heirloom — a ring my grandmother gave her when she graduated from high school. It was a striking rectangular ring with seven diamonds positioned diagonally. Framing both sides of the diamonds were rubies of a smaller size. The ring was oversized for my finger, so to give it a snugger fit, my mother wrapped Scotch tape around the underside of the band.

"Just wear it for special occasions, like going out to dinner," she told me. The next week we went out to Horn and Hardart, and after placing my order with the waitress, I slid out from the booth and raced down the spiral staircase to the restrooms. The bathroom was empty. I removed the ring and placed it beside the faucet on the pedestal sink, washed my hands, and ran back upstairs. As I sat down, my mother glanced down at my hand.

"Diana, where's the ring?"

Gasping, I slid out of the booth and bolted across the restaurant and back down the stairs to the bathroom. I searched everywhere — on the sink, in the drain and on the floor, but the ring was gone. The hostess and the manager also searched, but the ring never turned up.

"How could you do that?" my mother reprimanded. "Do you realize that your grandmother gave that ring to me? You should be ashamed of yourself." My mother was so angry that she never ate her dinner that evening.

∞

CHAPTER 4

Invasion of Galicia

By late August 1914, Austria-Hungary invaded Galicia. My grandmother, still eleven years old, recounts her memory of the day the soldiers walked into their town:

My sister Beronia and I shared a room, and we were both awakened to the clamor in the streets. My bed was near the window, and I immediately pulled open the curtains and looked down at the cobblestone road. The streetlights were all extinguished. Across the street in the blue and white houses, which looked just like ours, other families also pushed aside their curtains, wondering what the commotion was all about. What we saw were soldiers milling around the sidewalk right in front of our house!

I tossed the cover off my bed, adjusted the shoulder on my flannel nightgown, and ran down the corridor, trembling, to my parents' room.

"Mother, Father, come see what's going on downstairs in the street. I'm so scared," I said, tugging at my mother's arm. My father sat up in bed and turned to my mother and said:

"The Austro-Hungarian cavalries are on their way to the Russian border, just north of here."

All four of us gathered around our parents' bed waiting for either my mother or father to tell us what to do, but they were too stunned to utter one word. We clung onto our parents as if that gesture was the only way for us to survive. My father finally uttered the first words: "Things will change now in our town. The goal of these soldiers, children, is that in a few days, they will 'hash up' Russia."

The amazing thing to me was how the soldiers looked as if they could have been my brothers. I never wanted to think about my brothers being soldiers fighting in a war and the chance of them never returning home.

Whatever might have tossed around in my grandmother's mind, it is difficult for me to fathom the fear in a young girl's heart while witnessing the end of the peaceful world as she knew it. All of her daily rituals were sent into disarray and chaos surrounded her. I imagine this was very destabilizing in a young girl's life, and I speculate that the pressures of those years stayed with her for the rest of her life.

My grandmother shared her feelings about how her life began to change.

My patterns of waking up early in the morning, having breakfast, and walking to school were no longer a part of my daily routine. I still woke up at seven o'clock in the morning, but instead of going to school, I found myself wandering in circles around the house wondering what to do with myself. As it turned out, my only peace came when I decided to sit down to write. Writing relaxed me and made me feel better about what was going on in the world around me. There was really nothing else to do, because one by one, all the town's schools began closing.

One day at home, my grandmother and her siblings were reading in the living room when they were suddenly disturbed by a pandemonium in the street. The three of them hurried to the window and pushed the curtains aside to look outside. My grandmother explained:

The stream of soldiers marching through our ordinarily quiet street mesmerized me. My parents sat in the big plaid armchairs shaking their heads back and forth. I didn't understand what was happening, and this really frightened me. My mother finally broke the silence by saying, "How precarious is life. You just never know what to expect."

It was just so terrible that nobody had any time to prepare for the disaster. It seemed as if everyone ran in circles in their homes and on the streets, trying to figure out what to do next.

The Austro-Hungarian soldiers suddenly marched into our town as they were retreating from the advancing Russians. Their clothes were all torn up. They looked hungry and ate everything in sight. They took all the food from the stores, so when my mother went down for bread, there was none left. For hours, my parents stood in the streets holding out jars full of water. Eagerly, the soldiers grabbed them and nodded in thanks. Some even reached out to get a drink, yet they didn't even have a moment to sip it.

The soldiers gathered on a street corner. They were all dressed in long black coats with matching fur caps. I noticed that they had pouches of am-munition strapped across their chests. They also held these scary-looking swords that were raised up toward the heavens. They scared me out of my mind. I looked around and wondered what to do. It suddenly dawned on me to hide in the nearest doorway, in the hope that the Cossacks would not notice me.

I stood frozen in one spot, not wanting to draw any attention to my-self. From a neighboring building, I spotted a young boy about my sister's age. He was running alone into the deserted street.

The Cossacks watched him carefully. They then charged at him and began pounding him with their sticks. They took out their swords, and bit by bit began hacking him into small pieces. The boy yelled and screamed until there was no more little boy to make any more sounds.

I stood there paralyzed in fright and distraught at what lay before my eyes. My breaths made clouds around me in the frosty air. I had this urge to run out and help the boy, but I was afraid that the Cossacks would turn around and do the same to me. I wished I could vanish into the ground, become invisible, or run home completely unnoticed. I was too petrified to move and I didn't even know where to run to.

All of a sudden I turned around and saw a pretty young woman running toward the little boy. I assumed that it was his mother. She was wearing a casual dress and looked as if she'd been preparing dinner, be-cause her apron was slightly soiled. She ran toward her son yelling and screaming, "That's my son; that's my only son; what are you doing?"

As soon as they saw the boy's mother, the Cossacks began running away, but it was already too late; he was all chopped up. She cried relent-lessly as she bent down to pick up the pieces of her son on the blood-covered street. As she gathered every piece of her little boy, she howled at the top of her lungs. She then quickly put the pieces into her apron pockets, hoping that she would not be next.

I can hardly grasp what a deep impression this inci-dent must have left on my grandmother as a young girl. Our childhood wounds leave us with scars that most often never heal. The image of this young boy being hacked up in the street must be an image that my grandmother carried with her for the rest of her life. I can only imagine how someone can be haunted by witnessing such a horrific event. It also sickens me to think that the Cossacks could have done this to such a little boy living up the street from my grandmother. At one point, I thought how it could have been my grandmother who was hacked up, which means I would not have been here to tell her story. While reading this scene I also thought of the awful pain of losing a child. There is no pain like it. I miscarried once, and so I empathized with the woman's loss, even though my experience doesn't even closely parallel the horror she witnessed. It's impossible to fathom her anguish and sense of helplessness as she ran into the street to capture the pieces of her son. The emotional pain of losing a child surely lived with her forever, as has mine after my miscarriage.

After seeing what the Cossacks had done, my grandmother ran home to tell her parents.

I ran into the kitchen as my mother was preparing lunch, and I yelled, "Mom, Dad, you'll never believe what I just saw!"

"What?" my mother asked impatiently.

"You know that little blond boy Beronia's age that lives across from the grocery? You should see what they did to him! They killed him. They killed him in the worst possible way. Mom, Dad, I'm so scared to live here any more. Please let's leave."

My mother stood by the kitchen sink. After hearing my story, she began sobbing. She ran into her bedroom and frantically packed a few things into a bundle. My father walked into the room and admitted to my mother that it was time to leave.

"It's about time you agree with me," she yelled.

Unfortunately, because we waited so long to make our decision to leave, there were no longer any carts, carriages, or pushcarts left in the village. We had to make our getaway by holding in our arms all our most precious belongings.

In preparation for our departure, my father ran to the nearby store to buy some candles. On his way home, he stopped for a visit at a neighbor's house. He knocked on the door. No one answered. Timidly, he opened the door and peeked inside. His eyes rotated from left to right. He was stunned at what he saw. Corpses filled the entire apartment. Quickly, he slammed the door shut and ran home as fast as his feet would carry him. He insisted that we flee the horror afflicting our village. He said that we shouldn't even wait until the morning. As it turned out, the last train with fleeing soldiers left the day before, so we had to make our actual getaway on foot.

All six of us held hands and escaped to the outskirts of the town in the direction of where the Austrian army was retreating. We walked until our feet were ready to fall off.

I was so tired and hungry. The frustration was so intense. I had never felt anything like that in my life. My mouth felt like sandpaper, and the lining of my stomach turned into a knot. My hands trembled as I removed the strands of hair from my face.

None of us had any idea what, if anything, would become of us. We finally arrived at the neighboring village. There was not a person or a light on in the street. It was completely deserted and desolate. All the windows of the homes and stores were broken, and piles of garbage lined the streets. People had already fled from the oncoming Russian invasion. I stopped in the middle of the street and yelled out to my parents, "I told you we should have left earlier."

When we reached the outskirts of Galicia, we finally stumbled upon a hostel also occupied with others who had fled the Cossacks. With trepi-

dation, we walked into the cold cement building with large wooden doors. Together, we scanned the floor for an empty spot. After a few moments, we found one. We all lay down on a platform overseeing the road. We prayed for the next day to bring us a new dawn, a new beginning, and some peace, but it was a very restless night.

In the morning what I saw down below made my blood freeze. As far as our eyes could see, the Russian Army marched in the streets heading directly toward our hostel. My father told me that they weren't the Cossacks, but they were the regular infantry. The men inside the hostel said it was useless for us to escape. The head of the army entered the building and scanned us up and down and all around. The women and children sensed the heaviness of his stare and cried at the top of their lungs. The old men shook in fear that the army would take away their families and leave them behind. A deep relief permeated those in the building when a soldier told us that the children and older people were of no use to them. We were relieved when he told the rest of us to go home.

On our way back home, my mother confessed that she did not think she'd survive the events that would follow. She felt psychologically and physically drained by everything during the past few days. Once again, we arrived at the front of our house and could not believe our eyes. All of our belongings had been strewn all over the front yard. Rubbish had been thrown everywhere. We ran into the backyard, and the wooden shed door was flung open and its contents were tossed around the yard as if a tornado had spun. We all stood still and felt completely numb. Our home was in ruins. Almost everything that could be carried away was gone. Out of sight.

With trepidation, we returned to the front of the house and walked in. We ran from room to room examining the extent of the damage. Each room was worse than the previous one. Finally, we fell onto the living room floor. My father took some logs from the basket beside the fireplace and *tossed them inside for a fire. He then threw a few more logs into the stove in the kitchen. Slowly but surely, the house became warm again as it had been before we left.*

For a few months we returned to our daily routine. My brothers and sister and I returned to school, and my father went back to his work in the lumberyard.

Other eyewitness accounts share a somewhat different story concerning how Kalush was affected at the outset of the war. In his essay, Moyshe Ettinger writes:

> In 1914, at the outbreak of World War I, Kalush hung out the white flag of surrender, yielding the town to the Russians without a single shot being fired. The police changed into civilian clothes. Reif, the Jewish policeman, whose nickname was Madalondra, the former Austrian horn player, suddenly looked broken and pathetic, and stripped of his glory. Whoever was able, fled the town, and those who remained waited anxiously, their hearts filled with dread, for the Russian troops, not knowing what fate awaited them. But the Russians occupied Kalush peaceably; several weeks later a large Russian army marched through the streets of the town, reaching for the Carpathian Mountains, confident that they would effortlessly conquer the capital city of Austria — Vienna — and the war would be over.

According to my grandmother's journal, the peace and order did not last long. In the spring of 1915, when she was twelve years old, chaos erupted once again on the streets of Galicia.

One day, with her small allotment of flour, my mother decided to bake enough bread for the entire week. While the bread was baking in the oven, she heard a noise sounding like hail smashing against their roof. She looked outside, but it wasn't even raining, plus we never had hail in the spring. In a short time, she realized that what she was hearing was the sound of live ammunition. For protection, we all ran downstairs to the cellar, because thank goodness we had already gathered some emergency food and supplies down there. We left the cellar door ajar.

As we sat down on the floor, I looked up on the stairs and spotted a soldier's feet moving down the stairs. Another pair of feet came into view and collapsed near the top of the stairs. I looked down and saw blood dripping onto the stairs. With me tailing closely behind, my mother dashed up the wide set of stairs and stepped over a dead soldier to remove the bread from the oven.

We stayed in the house while my father dragged the dead soldier outside to the front lawn. The cellars in those days were made up of many secret passages and coves and a lot of scary places for people to hide. Those places became even more eerie during wartime. My father ordered all five of us to stay in the cellar until further notice. We all huddled together, scared to move and uncertain about the events that would follow. We remained in the cellar until the next day, when a neighbor finally came knocking on our door.

"Good news," the neighbor said, "the Cossacks were driven out of the village. The Austrian army is on its way back."

With glee, we rushed up the basement stairs and immediately dashed outside. The streets were jammed with residents rejoicing because of the return of the Austrian army. Heaps of unburied bodies lay every-where. Panic was rampant. During the next little while, the warm weather arrived, and with it came a sudden outbreak of Asian cholera. Almost immediately, the city officials executed rules to minimize any further spread of the disease. The schools remained closed, and nobody was per-mitted to shake hands or even exchange money. To prevent getting cholera, some village citizens walked around with bags of camphor strung around their necks.

CHAPTER 5

Cholera Strikes

My grandmother describes the horrors of war, disease, and loss she witnessed in 1915:

One day when I was about twelve years old, I woke up and decided to go for an early morning walk. After some time, I got tired and collapsed on a wooden bench outside the grocery store. I fell asleep. An hour later, I woke up yelling and screaming. I popped up like a jack-in-the-box and looked around. I had dreamt that my mother was dying. Nervous and frightened, I got up from the bench and quickly ran back home. My mother came to the door and asked what was wrong, but I did not answer. She brought me into the kitchen and grudgingly offered me a warm drink. I was so distraught about the bad dream that I ended up pushing the drink out of my mother's hand. My mother's dress and the kitchen floor became soaked with water. Feeling even more annoyed, my mother kept asking why I was crying. I was too petrified to tell her. So instead, I ran to my room crying, with my mother trailing behind, slapping me and trying to get an answer from me.

My grandmother was a good daughter, and every day she made a point of kissing her parents good-bye when she left for school and saying hello when she returned home at the end of the day. The day after her dream, she came home from school and the house was quieter than usual. She called for her parents, but there was no answer.

After dashing in and out of a few rooms, I finally heard my mother's faint voice calling me from her bedroom. I walked in and my mother slowly sat up in her bed and complained that she was not feeling well. She said she was nauseous and had been vomiting all day. I glanced over to my father, who was not usually in bed in the middle of the afternoon; he was sound asleep next to her. He also looked pale, and I noticed that in his sleep his hands were trembling.

Mortified and filled with disbelief, my eyes looked back and forth from my mother to my father. I feared the worst.

A few days earlier, I had heard from neighbors that cholera had already begun to spread through our entire village. They spoke about the problems at school, and the local newspapers reminded us not to drink the water unless it was boiled. We were also told to eat only food that had been thoroughly cooked. The rule was to boil it, cook it, and peel it.

I could not believe how awful my parents looked. I gave out a scream at the top of my lungs. I was petrified. I sensed that my horrible dream of the night before was about to come true.

Finally, my mother got up from bed and went to sit on the sofa in the living room. She sat there for a few minutes before curling up and vomit-

ing out of control. She sat up grasping her stomach and yelling for help. My father woke up and came running, and so did my brothers. For hours we all tried to alleviate her pain by bringing her warm drinks and hot towel compresses to her forehead. It was evident that she was very sick with cholera. Her stomach could not hold anything, not even a little glass of water or brandy. Neither doctors nor disinfectants were available. According to the posters plastered all over town, all the sick people had to be removed. The small hospital couldn't hold all those sick people.

I was so worried about my father and the possibility that he might lose his wife and be left with us four children to take care of. He was so helpless. For the rest of the day, he dragged himself around the house, slippers shuffling beneath him. He didn't shave and was not hungry. He forced himself to come to the table for meals, and when he finally arrived, he wore a catatonic expression, as if my mother had already died.

My father used to be very enthusiastic and emotional about politics and would easily be involved in long discussions with his friends in the living room. He no longer felt like doing that.

He was so dependent upon my mother. He had absolutely no idea about how a house should be run. He was a strong believer that attending the house was strictly a woman's job. He was clumsy in the kitchen and had no idea how to do the laundry. Once when my mother was ill, he tried to help but ended up breaking almost every dish in the kitchen and burning all the meals. "Your mind is elsewhere," my mother used to tell him.

For twenty-four hours, my father tried to conceal my mother's illness from everyone else in the village. He was afraid that if people found out, they might decide to quarantine all of us in the family, and this frightened him more than anything.

That night he sent all of us kids to stay at a friend's house. He told us that he needed a break. He reminded us to keep it a secret that our mother *was ill. If the neighbors found out we were contagious, they would change their minds and not allow us to spend the night.*

All four of us kissed our parents good-bye, ran out the door and up the street as fast as our feet could carry us. As I ran, the gruesome images of my recent nightmare flashed before me. At the friend's house that evening, I tossed and turned on the mattress set on the floor — unable to close my eyes and fall asleep.

I stared up at the ceiling wondering what life might be like without a mother, "even if your mother never wanted you," I thought.

At the friend's house the following morning, I woke up to a shoulder nudge. I rolled over and looked up and saw the friend's pale face. The woman, wearing a long black dress and embroidered apron, stood stiffly staring down at me. Her face was expressionless and cold.

"Your mother has been taken to the hospital. The rest of the family must be quarantined."

I could not move. I lay still in bed. I knew that my bad dream was about to come true.

"You better get moving," said the woman. "You cannot stay here anymore."

In her journal, my grandmother didn't describe her departure from that home or the quarantine experience. But reports tell us that the practice of quarantine began back in the fourteenth century to protect coastal cities from plague epidemics. When ships arrived in Venice from infected ports, they were required to sit in quarantine at the port for at least forty days. The word "quarantine" is derived from the Latin word *quaresma*, meaning forty.

I haven't had any experience with quarantine, but I imagine it's a dreadful experience. The closest I came to separating the ill from the healthy was while bedside nursing in the cardiac surgery unit in the 1980s. To sequester those with postoperative wound infections, they were placed in protective isolation. A big red sign hung on their door beside a shelf holding masks, booties, and gloves, which had to be worn by anyone entering the room — janitors, nurses, doctors, and visitors. Bright red plastic bags were used for the garbage gathered from those rooms. They were disposed of separately and under very strict surveillance.

I remember speaking with one gentleman in isolation. He was a CEO for a local bank, and while changing his bandage, I asked him how he was and he just poured out his heart. "You know, it's very depressing in this room. I feel untouchable. This is a difficult situation for someone who's busy and always involved with people. You just feel like poison being here in this room. You feel completely contaminated. It's so dreadful," he told me.

We can never really understand what it's like to be in quarantine or in isolation unless we are so unfortunate to experience it ourselves.

My grandmother wrote this the following day after her mother was taken to the hospital to be quarantined:

> It was four o'clock in the morning and everyone was sound asleep. I quietly got dressed and tiptoed outside the hostel searching for the whereabouts of my mother. I had not slept well at all. Images of my mother infiltrated my mind, and her ghost suspended all around the room. I walked a few blocks on the cobblestone streets lit by streetlights. The streets were completely empty except for this one rat rummaging around in the garbage in front of the grocery store. At the end of the village was a big open field.
>
> I knew that the infirmary was on the other side of that field. With

bare feet, I trotted over the green fields, every so often lifting my foot up to remove a pebble caught between my toes. Small and large trees were scattered throughout the field. I moved my flashlight around to help identify any scary nighttime creatures.

I approached the building just as the sun poked its face over the horizon. The outside of the building was barren; there were no trees immediately surrounding it, but there was a rather high fence that I could not jump over. I wondered why an infirmary had to be fenced in. The people inside were too sick to escape. Anyway, why would they want to leave if they were not feeling well?

At the far corner of the building stood a guard with his bayonets pointing straight up in the air, diligently guarding the fenced-in property. I sensed that he would not allow me inside. As I walked toward him, he turned the corner of the building. As soon as I couldn't see him anymore, I ran quickly along the edge of the fence. I glanced over and noticed an opening in the fence and quickly wiggled my body through. When I arrived at the other side, I looked left and right and then dashed into the long cement building.

I tiptoed inside, as if they could hear my bare feet walking. There was no one near the door. I found this strange, especially since there was a serious-looking guard outside. As far as my eyes could see, the halls inside were lined with rows and rows of occupied beds. There was talking, but I did not understand any of it. Older people were lying in their beds acting delirious and speaking in rambling nonsense. Others lay in their beds completely still. I wondered if the ones who were not moving were either dead or asleep. They all looked so pale, it was hard to tell.

The concrete walls of the building had this incredibly cold and distant feel about them. I looked down and saw the stone floor covered with straw. There were not enough beds for the number of bodies in that room. Bodies were piled up on top of the straw. Some parts of the floor were slip-

pery and entirely coated with vomit. I staggered down the hall and finally stumbled and fell. A dark-haired woman lying on the floor squirmed in my direction, grabbed my arm, and hung onto it. I tried to shake her off. I pulled myself back onto my feet and continued the search for my mother. Another woman yanked at my long dress, repeatedly begging for water. I kept walking ahead, weaving in and out of the bodies, desperately trying not to step on them. To my horror, every face looked exactly like the one of my mother's.

After wandering and searching in vain for an hour, I decided to give up the search for my mother. I felt emotionally drained by seeing all the un-claimed and ill people. The sun was already high up over the horizon. I walked outside the infirmary looking for the same hole in the fence that got me inside, but could not find it. Again I saw the guard at the corner of the building, and so I scrambled in the opposite direction, crouching down along the fence in an effort to camouflage myself. Finally, the guard turned around and spotted me. He ran toward me waving his bayonet in the air and cursing something in German. I desperately searched for the hole in the fence. When I found it, I slipped through and ran as fast as my feet would carry me. The guard never caught me, but kept yelling something in German that I did not understand.

Halfway back to the hostel I stopped to rest and catch my breath. I sat down under a shaded tree in the middle of the field. I was completely drained of energy. To me it seemed as if I'd been crying and praying for two days straight. With my back leaning against the tree trunk and my legs extended straight out, I stared back at the infirmary. I wanted to be-lieve that my mother was still alive somewhere inside the building, but bleakness overcame me.

One part of me wanted to run back and look again for the face of my mother, yet another part of me was absolutely terrified to find her. I pulled a tissue out of my apron pocket and then the only photo I ever had of my mother. She was seated on the porch mending socks, the same spot where she told me that I should become a doctor one day. I remembered feeling so warmed by her words and wondered if I'd ever again get that feeling or see the face of my mother again. A tear dropped on my tissue. I was overwhelmed by feelings of loneliness in my journey to find my mother. I desperately wished somebody was with me. Feelings of isolation and frustration grasped me, and I finally decided the best decision would be to return to the hostel where my brothers and father waited.

She wrote this the following morning:

As six o'clock in the morning approached, the sun made its way above the horizon. I stood up, stretched out my arms toward the heavens and glanced down at my dirty feet. In an effort to keep warm, I hugged myself. On the way back to the hostel from the infirmary, I had walked along the fence toward the mortuary on the other side of the field. The building looked similar to the infirmary except it had only two windows, one on either side. As I approached the building, one part of me wanted to rush inside, yet another part of me was absolutely horrified.

There were no guards or fences outside the mortuary. The door was wide open. I entered and stood at the doorway while my eyes shifted from left to right. Corpses were lying on the floor covered in their own garments. It seemed to me that in the distance I saw my mother's black skirt lying over a body. There was a brush-like trim on the bottom seam, just like my mother's. I was sure it was her. As I began walking toward the bodies, a worker approached me, motioning for me to come to the information desk.

I staggered to the wooden desk. A nun sat stiffly behind it. I told her I was looking for my mother. She assured me that my mother was sick, but that she would eventually be fine. But in my heart I knew she was lying to me and that my mother's body was somewhere in that immense room. I *knew too well that there was no mother for me anymore. The nun implored me to go home. I walked slowly back through the field, feeling no sense of resolve from my morning journey. When I arrived back at the hostel, I plunked down on my bed. My family had already woken up and gone out somewhere. I had little energy to look for them or begin my day and all the chores I had to do. Nothing mattered to me any more.*

By the end of the day, we all returned home. A few days later there was a knock on our front door.

"Good morning, Regina," said Mrs. Stern. "I have come to tell you that your father is quarantined and cannot attend the viewing of your mother. If you want to see her before she's buried in a mass grave, then you need to come with me now. If not, you'll never see her again."

My grandmother refused to go. In her journal she didn't explain why. I can only imagine that she was scared and tired as a result of the recent events. There's also the possibility of her denying that her nightmare was about to come true. Unfortunately it did. At the age of twelve, my grandmother was forced into running the household with her eight-year-old sister. Their grandmother was too old to look after her and her sister, and their two older brothers had already made plans to leave for Vienna in search of a new job and a new life. Her father was also too ill emotionally and physically to look after the girls.

In the winter of 1915–1916, my school reopened. Each day I attended school, did my homework and carried out household tasks. When nighttime arrived, I collapsed in bed. With each day I noticed my father became even more depressed. For hours he sat in his armchair in a semi-catatonic state. He spoke very little; I had to pull words out of him. He ate very little. I tried preparing homemade meals. His grief sapped his appetite for food and for life. I tried wrapping my arms around him, hoping my love could penetrate and heal his soul. He was a stern person who had never been approachable. Somehow, this was the first time he ever let me touch him.

I was a very light sleeper. I would hear my father wake up during the middle of the night and walk around in a stupor. He wandered down the hall and around the apartment. With no explanation or destination, he would return to his room again. One evening he popped up in bed and reached for a cigarette on his bedside table. More than once, he accidentally set his bed on fire by falling asleep still holding a cigarette. One night when everyone else (except for me) was sound asleep, he got dressed and wandered into the street. Without him knowing it, I got dressed and followed him. He began roaming the sleeping neighborhood. Suddenly a few blocks away he did an about face and turned back home on his own. We both arrived at the front door at the same time. He was surprised to see me and also a little bit mad.

When not chasing my father, I read in bed until late at night. Sometimes I woke up early in the morning to study. Each morning before school, I washed my face and put on my uniform — a navy blue skirt with a huge safety pin on the side, white blouse, knee-high socks, and Oxford shoes. I was happy at school. My teachers were so nice to me. When I didn't turn in my assignments, they tapped me on the back and said it would be okay to turn them in when they were ready.

CHAPTER 6

Escape From Galicia

In 1916, after her mother's death, my grandmother continued to juggle her domestic and academic responsibilities, but the political calm did not last long.

Once again we heard the rumbling of cannons coming our way. I didn't think I could live through it again. All of us ran outside and put our ears to the soil. The sound of marching feet got louder and louder by the moment. The Russians were returning. This second time around, we did not believe anything we read in the newspapers. We only trusted our ears and our instincts. Rumors began spreading that the Russian enemies were approaching our village. I asked my father whether we should pack our belongings so that we would be prepared to run away. With an expression of helplessness, he stretched his arms out. He wanted to say something, but then covered his face with his hands. Whatever illness he had had taken over all his faculties. He had difficulty communicating. Things were very different this time than they were during the last invasion. My mother was gone. We packed and packed for two days, and every little nothing seemed important to my father. I was such a young child and did not know how to stop my father from crying and sobbing all day long. He cried so much he could hardly speak. From the linen closet I grabbed some sturdy sheets and sewed them together to make a big sack. Inside the sack I placed our clothes, linens, and all of my mother's dresses.

The next day my father, my sister, and I followed the streams of residents in the direction of the train station. Some people had already been sleeping there for days on their bales of belongings. The entire town gathered there to get away from the Russians. We sat all day waiting for a train to arrive. By evening the train had still not pulled into the train station. Totally exhausted, we all flopped down onto our sacks and fell asleep. Just as the sun came over the horizon, a train filled with passengers pulled into the station. Everyone stood up in the expectation that this would be the train to take us away, but quickly we learned that it was packed like sardines from door to door with retreating soldiers. With longing and saddened eyes, we and all the other people watched as it pulled away.

Soon after, rumors spread throughout the village that another train would soon arrive, but we didn't want to build up any hopes only to be disappointed once again. With escalating feelings of dread, we waited and waited. Finally, ten hours later, much to our surprise a freight train pulled in.

We didn't care that it was a freight train. We pushed ourselves on anyway. We tossed our sacks and bags over our heads. My father was too weak to lift his. People rushed and tugged in all directions, and someone had the nerve to approach me from behind and tear the skirt off my body. I stood in my underpants crying and praying to the high heavens that things would get better, because they certainly could not get any worse.

After being on the train for an hour, in the distance I noticed my

*young and chic schoolteacher — the one who had taken me under her
wing just after my mother died. She stood at the train's entrance laughing
and smiling with some young good-looking officers. Staring in my direction, she whispered something to them and then pointed toward me. Before
having a chance to realize what was happening, they ran toward my sister
and me and grabbed our sacks. One of the officers lifted me onto his shoulders. The other one did the same with my sister. I screamed and pointed toward my father. While being ushered away, I noticed another officer
bringing my father onto the train.*

*My teacher came toward us and whispered in my ear that she prom-
ised to look over me. She told me that I could always count on her. She said
she would do anything in her power to make sure everything turned out
right. In my heart I had difficulty believing that our situation could get
much worse. I looked down at the floor of the train and saw it was coated
in straw. It reminded me of the day I went to look for my mother in the infirmary. I felt sick to my stomach. The train had no washing or toilet facil-
ities. In all, we were forty-six men, women, and children. For an arduous
three and one-half weeks, we called that train our home.*

*Once in a while the train stopped at countryside stations. We all
scurried off the train and charged to nearby toilets, slurped on some water
at the fountains, and ate bread and soup from the generous army field
kitchens. By the time September 1916 rolled around, the weather turned
extremely cold.*

Finally the train came into the station in Moravia,
where there was a camp for the evacuees in Ungarisch-
Hradisch, a Jewish community. This was a region in
Czechoslovakia of only 10,076 square miles. Shortly before the end of World War I, the Independent Republic
of Czechoslovakia was established, with Moravia as one
of its provinces. During World War II, German troops

occupied this region. In 1945, the United States and Soviet forces drove the German troops out.

My grandmother continued to describe the train saga:

> *Unfortunately, the train did not receive clearance to stop at the Moravia station. There were too many people who wanted to board the train and there was not enough room. After three days, those who were already on the train, including my family, were unloaded further along the railway track. We stayed in temporary barracks that had been used by railway repairmen. The conditions were miserable. There was no water, food, or heat. A group of men walked to the next village to tell its residents about all of us needing a place to live. Within minutes, a slew of women arrived at the barracks to fetch children to bring into their homes. Others were given shelter in a deserted brick factory situated on the top of a distant hill. We lost contact with our father on the train and didn't know where he was. An older hunchback widow with a floral scarf on her head approached my sister and me and asked if we wanted to come stay with her.*
>
> *I could not pass up the offer to live in a real home with real people. We both bowed at the old lady and gave her a big hug. She carried two bundles of food and we offered to help her. With smiles on our faces, we walked with her to her home.*
>
> *She brought us into her small villa a few minutes away from the station and turned us over to the maid to be fed and washed. I was thrilled to have finally received such personalized care. The maid was about to undress us when she stopped short and ran out of the bedroom. We sat staring at one another, not knowing what we had done. Outside the door the maid whispered something to the lady.*

The maid came back and took us out on the verandah and told us to take off all our clothes. She watched as we threw every piece of our clothing into the furnace. We were absolutely sown with lice. Beronia and I had become used to this condition and simply couldn't understand their fuss and ado about it.

It did not take long before many others settled in the brick factory not far from this woman's house. Within a few days the officials announced that there was a major outbreak of typhoid fever. When the lady heard about the outbreak of typhoid fever, she returned us to the barracks where we came from. She said that she did not want anything to do with us. Once again we felt abandoned and left to fend for ourselves.

During the day we wandered the streets until we spotted a sign offering accommodations. We knocked on the door. The homeowner, an old, short, and balding gentleman with a limp and wearing a brown suit, welcomed us into the small foyer. In the corner was a table with a stained-glass lamp and a black dial telephone. The wooden floors were covered with older Persian rugs whose fringes had knotted over time.

After scanning us up and down, the gentleman said he could provide us with a room offering the bare essentials — a bed, a night table, and a reading light. Beronia and I looked at one another and nodded. We asked to take a look at it first. We followed the man up the narrow wooden stairwell with a thick wooden banister. He turned left into a small room with two single beds. In the corner was a small washing sink and a small towel rack on the wall. The window with its white sheer curtains overlooked the main street. The beds were made with a red and white quilt, and a matching Persian rug lay across the wooden floor. We whispered to each other and agreed that it was a good enough place to stay warm and get a good night's sleep. We had no energy to look further for what might have been a more suitable accommodation.

After putting our sacks in our new room, we went downstairs to ask the man where we could take a long walk. After getting directions, we ended up in the center of the village and made it a point to keep a safe distance from the other residents in the village. We were petrified of becoming infected with typhoid. While on our walk, we had to go to the bathroom, yet were too scared to use public toilets, so we waited until we saw a field and squatted behind the bushes.

We returned a few hours later to our accommodation to borrow a basket from the gentleman. We decided to go berry picking in the large field behind the house. When the pickings became slim, we roamed farther away from the house. Beronia and I ended up wandering down different rows. About half an hour later, I looked up wanting to compare my berry collection with Beronia's.

In the distance, I noticed Beronia tottering as if she were drunk. I stared for a moment and then ran toward her. I shook her and asked what was wrong. "Nothing," she replied. But I did not believe her. I dragged her all the way to the man's house.

The man was not there, so all by myself I dragged my sister up the stairs and tucked her into bed. I went to the sink and applied a cold washcloth to her forehead. Beronia slept for many hours. In the early evening she woke up yelling for water. I gave her as much as she could tolerate.

No doctor wanted to enter our area. I tried to cool Beronia's head with more cloths soaked in ice water. I lay down beside her, trying to capture some of her heat, but to no avail. Somehow my father found us in that house. I do not know how. When he arrived at the front door he was in a state of delirium. He nearly collapsed at the front door. It looked as if he had spent his last bit of energy finding us. We soon learned that he had been quarantined and was just allowed to leave because they had too many people who were more ill than him.

I walked my father to the sofa and laid him down. It seemed as if the entire house was being turned into an infirmary, and it was not even my house. My father lay on the sofa staring into space. It was impossible to carry on a conversation with him. He did not utter a word. He turned to stone in crises like these.

I didn't know what to do. Night arrived, and I stood looking out the living room window watching the trains arrive at the station at the foot of the hill. We so badly wanted to leave the village. But ever since typhoid fever had broken out, barbed wire was put all around the area, absolutely forbidding our leaving. My sister began talking even more deliriously, talk that made no sense at all. I was in some situation.

One night, just after midnight, when Beronia and my father were sound asleep, I grabbed my winter coat and gathered water, a pen, and a pad of paper into a bag. I tiptoed outside and slipped through the wire fence surrounding the area and made my way to the dimly lit train station. People were everywhere waiting for the arrival of the next train. I sat down on a stone and wrote about our predicament. Writing was my only means of survival. I really had no one to talk to. I had no one to help us find a solution to our predicament. My sister and father were helpless, and it was obvious that I had to take control of the entire situation. My frustrations poured out through my pen.

While writing, I was disturbed by the sound of a fast-moving train heading in my direction. I looked up, and within moments the train stopped at the station and crowds of people from the other side of the track piled on.

With envy and tears in my eyes, I stared at the departing train packed with passengers. I waved, but not one person lifted a hand to wave back. Like I had done after leaving the mortuary, I brought my knees to the ground and my hands to my heart, begging to be taken away, somewhere, anywhere. Shivering in my mother's long coat, I sat back down on the stone. I contemplated my future and what to do. More than anything else *in the world, I wanted to see my brother Herman in Vienna. I needed to get out of the village, so infested with sick people with no cures and nowhere to go. So many of them just accepted what was happening to them, but I refused to do that.*

I became enticed by the idea of living in a real home again — some place where I did not have any worries and could be a child again. When the train pulled away, I flipped to a new page and wrote a note to my brother Herman, who told me he was living somewhere in Vienna.

Dear Herman:

> *You have no idea what we have been through and the conditions we have lived under and continue to live under. Beronia and I have wandered the streets looking for a safe place to be live, free from harm and disease. We badly want to live in a real home with a real family. We do not need much, just a warm place to sleep and some food to eat. We could be at your doorstep within a week. Please, brother Herman, hear our pain. Please accept us.*

> *Love,*
> *Your sister, Reggie*

A few days later Regina was thrilled to receive a letter from Herman in the mail:

Dear Reggie:

> *It's so nice to hear from you. I understand what you have been through. It's not an easy situation in both Moravia and Vienna. You should know that Vienna does not easily admit evacuees. They are afraid of any epidemics and diseases*

you might bring with you. Plus, the government has no extra food, shelter, or heat. The police closely guard the train stations, and it is entirely too risky for you to take the trip.

Love,

Herman

Here are my grandmother's comments after receiving Herman's letter:

I held the letter in my hand for a few moments before placing it in my sack. I just don't understand how my own brother, my own flesh and blood, could ignore my plea. What kind of witch was he married to that they couldn't offer to help us? It's all her fault. Our family never behaved like this. I remember my mother used to tell me about how sons become one with their wives, sometimes to the detriment of their blood family. I don't even know the woman and I detest her.

CHAPTER 7

Orphaned in Vienna

By late 1916, Beronia slowly recovered from her illness. As soon as her strength returned, my grandmother decided that in spite of their brother Herman's objection, they would both leave Kalush and make their way to Vienna. From an early age, my grandmother had a certain intuition about the way things should and could be. She was a doer and a fixer, and she sensed that there was little hope for them to remain in Galicia.

Actually, she was not the only one who thought this way. By the time Beronia recovered, many other Galician Jews were beginning to flee to Vienna.

My grandmother, now thirteen years old, wrote about her predicament:

With my mother now gone and my brothers in Vienna, there was nothing keeping us in Galicia except the memories, which were becoming more painful with each passing day. My father resisted our moving away. He was mortified by the prospect of any sort of change. He said he was afraid first of traveling and then of dying. Somehow I was able to convince him that it was a good idea to leave town.

"What will happen if we get caught leaving the camp?" he asked me over and over again. I patiently told him that I didn't have all the answers, but I just knew that it was time to leave Galicia. So we packed our bags, sneaked away from the camp, and made our way to the nearby train station.

My grandmother continued:

The train finally pulled into the station. I pushed my still weakened sister up onto the train platform and a soldier pulled her inside. I followed. My father entered another car. We avoided clumping together so that nobody would suspect that we were escaping the camp. On the far end of the train, a soldier was sprawled out on a bench, sleeping. Because my sister was still too weak to stand for long periods of time, I placed her beside him, leaning against him on the bench. He soon woke up grumbling and then motioned for Beronia to sit down. Within a few minutes my sister was completely stretched out in his place. The train raced through the night.

I could not fall asleep. My eyes moved along watching the passing fields, spotting an occasional home with lights glaring inside the windows. Filled with envy, I fantasized about the prospects of having a safe place to live, a place to lay my head safely down. I wanted to continue with all the good in my life. I especially wanted to finish school. I was getting tired of this state of perpetual survival — running from one shelter to the next.

At noon the following day, the train came to a halt. All the passengers rushed out. I dragged my sister behind me while scanning the platform left and right for our father. We wondered if one more time we had *been abandoned. I noticed the police had blocked all the exits. Before allowing the passengers to disembark, they carefully looked over every man, requesting his military papers. My sister and I kept moving with the crowd, ducking under the elbows of the grown-ups.*

By November 1916, my grandmother and her sister stood on the pavement of Vienna in front of Ostbahnhof, Vienna's East Station. According to my research, all trains arriving from the south and the east ended up at that station. My grandmother had heard that Vienna was the center of music, art, and literature, and this excited her. By this time, she had lost all contact with her father. She had no idea where he ended up.

She wrote this about their first day in Vienna:

As soon as we stepped off the train onto Viennese soil, I realized how little German I spoke. I barely understood what the conductor said as he helped us off the train. I smiled at him and then followed the crowds of people in the direction of what I thought was the street. We stumbled on an information booth and asked in Polish about the direction to the trolley car. The woman saw that we spoke very little German and called over a coworker to translate. We were then directed to the entrance of a trolley car.

Holding only one old brown suitcase each, we walked lopsidedly and climbed the trolley's stairs. The woman conductor in a blue uniform and hat stood at the top of the stairs and extended her hand, motioning for our fare. Not knowing what else to do or say, we held up all we had — our railroad tickets. With pity in her eyes, the conductor scrutinized us up and down and motioned us inside. We smiled back and lowered our hands as we staggered up the aisle to find two seats at the back of the trolley.

After five minutes, I left Beronia and the bags and wandered to the front of the trolley, grabbing onto the seat handles as I walked. When the trolley came to a halt, I showed the conductor the envelope with my brother's address. The conductor nodded. I returned to my seat, and at the next stop the conductor looked in the rearview mirror and motioned us forward. When we got to the front of the trolley, the conductor placed her arms around both of our shoulders, pointing out the trolley's front window and up the street in the direction of Herman's house. We walked off the trolley and glanced back at the conductor, who smiled and tipped her hat to us.

My grandmother recapped her sentiments after getting off the trolley in Vienna:

As the trolley pulled away, we stood frozen on the Vienna street. We could see by those in the neighborhood that it was the Jewish quarter, because there were many rabbinic-looking people with prayer books wandering the streets. I stopped for a moment to reflect upon the Shabbat dinners my mother used to prepare on Friday evenings and how the guests had to kiss her hand when they entered. I thought about our father, who, before his mother died, was a rabbi and how he talked about fasting every Monday and Thursday for what he said was to please God. My mother used to joke about this, saying that he fasted because it was wartime and they didn't have enough food.

I glanced down at the paper with Herman's address. I suddenly felt overwhelmed with uncertainty about what lay ahead. Beronia was still so weak, so I pulled her along with one hand and with the other hand held the suitcase and Herman's house number.

We finally arrived at Herman's house. We stopped in front of the house, and looked it up and down wondering if this would be our new home. We climbed three flights of stairs to the front door. My brother's wife, Lilly, opened the door, and without even uttering a hello, she called out: "What bad spell brought you here?" I stopped in my tracks and didn't move forward. How did she even know who I was? She spoke with a voice full of anger. "Do not let the cold air in. We have no coal. Get the devil inside," she continued.

She directed us into the living room and told us that our brother was at work at the haberdashery. We both sat down and waited for what seemed like too many hours until our brother arrived home in the evening. Being in the house with that witch was the longest day of my life. She offered us only water to drink. She didn't offer us an iota of food or even a substantial drink. We could tell by her mannerisms and expressions that she was not enthusiastic about having us. We felt like an additional burden.

My grandmother added:

Just before Herman walked through the door, I wandered outside for a late afternoon stroll. Restaurants and cafés were scattered throughout the residential community. The main street was lit up as bright as day. On one corner there was a rather large café partly indoors and partly outdoors. The patrons inside were laughing and drinking and some were dancing to live music. Others sat outside at tables, smoking unfiltered cigarettes. The ashtrays overflowed with half-smoked cigarettes while all the happy people sipped their drinks and laughed loudly. I propped myself up against the wall at the edge of the building. I stared at the people inside the cafe.

I couldn't believe my eyes. All the gaiety was beyond my comprehension. How could the world be so divided? In one part people laughed, and danced, yet in another part people lived without hope, light, and food, but only with a sense of death and destruction. "Truly, God, so far above, it's hard to understand your ways." I sobbed and sobbed relentlessly until it was time to return home.

She commented on the rest of the afternoon:

We spent the rest of the afternoon sitting and waiting in the living room for our brother to return from work. We did not take our eyes off the front door. We sat talking about what we had been through as thirteen-and nine-year-olds. It was so hard to believe! When we spotted Herman walking through the front door, we immediately ran and flung ourselves into his arms. He dropped his briefcase, and in each arm he lifted us up and swung us around. He then asked if we were hungry, and we both gave a solid nod. In each hand he took us into the kitchen and sat us down at the kitchen table. He turned to the refrigerator and took out some meat, potatoes, and carrots. He stuck them all in a pot and made us a big bowl of soup. Lilly made a cameo appearance, reminding us to put napkins on our laps, and then disappeared into some back room. Again, I sensed her coldness and unwelcoming air, but somehow I was used to women who couldn't show much affection.

In her journal my grandmother no longer mentioned what happened to their father. I'm not sure what became of him. I interviewed the few remaining relatives, and there was some speculation of his whereabouts. Supposedly he had moved to Israel to be with my grandmother's eldest brother, Willy. It's unclear how long he lived there or what he did there. Through my mother, I know that Willy was a high official in the Israeli Postal System in Tel Aviv and was very close to my grandmother. His daughter's name was Derora and she was unable to have children, and adopted two girls, the eldest of whom was diagnosed with schizophrenia in her late twenties. As therapy, Derora taught her how to do needlepoint. She ended up creating incredible wall hangings, one of which hung in the prime minister of Israel's office. On my recent visit there, I bought that wall hanging and now it hangs on our living room wall.

My grandmother wrote this after spending a night at Herman's:

> *The following morning, after a good night's sleep, Herman took Beronia and me to find a suitable apartment. We walked up and down the streets of Vienna hunting for one of the few remaining vacancies. So many people had immigrated and there were not many spaces available. For hours, we knocked on door after door looking for a place to live. Finally, just before the sun set, we found a suitable furnished dwelling. It was located just outside the banking district. It had the bare essentials — two beds, a table to eat on, and an old living room sofa.*

My grandmother comments after a week in Vienna:

> *After about a week, I called my brother to say that we did not feel welcomed in our apartment building. The Viennese did not welcome evacuees, even if they were children. Nobody pitied us or tried to help us. Just like everyone else in the community, we had to wait in long lines to get food for the day. For hours Beronia and I lined up at the town's markets waiting for our small ration of milk, bread, and coal. A few times during the day, I felt like going out into the middle of the street and yelling at the top of my lungs, but my sister urged me not to. So instead, I waited patiently in line and refrained from uttering a word to anyone. I thought that because I was a child, they'd become even more angry and impatient with*

me. A part of me believed that the Viennese people did not particularly like children and didn't respect us as much as they did back in Galicia. Although I didn't regret leaving Galicia, there were days when I wondered if it would eventually become easier for us to live in Vienna in an orphanage.

And after two weeks in Vienna:

One morning, about two weeks after arriving in Vienna, I walked to the corner store to buy some milk. When I arrived, I noticed that there were no lines and that the shelves were completely empty. In my broken German, I asked the storekeeper when the next shipment will arrive. Uncaringly, he shrugged his shoulders. I returned home, and in desperation I knocked on our neighbor's door.

An elderly woman opened the blue-paneled door and smiled.

"Hello, my name is Regina. I live next door and we don't have any milk. I wondered if you had some to spare."

As soon as the woman heard my broken German accent, her face dropped. She put her hands on her hips on the band of her apron and said: "This is ridiculous, this huge infiltration of evacuees arriving from all parts of the monarchy into Vienna. Who do these people think they are?"

She turned around to her husband sitting at the kitchen table nursing a cup of coffee and said: "They come here, eat our food and use our supplies."

Without a moment's hesitation, the woman spit in my face and slammed the door. Dumbfounded, I stood outside staring at the door while listening to her mutter painful words about the evacuees to her husband.

"They should all be sent back to where they came from, those damned people and their talk dripping with accents. Nobody needs them; nobody invited them. They just make our lines grow longer and longer," she told him.

I slowly returned to our apartment, with my head hanging low in the disbelief that things could be so bad. All I wanted to do was to curl up and die. It seemed as if since my mother died, nothing had gone my way.

My grandmother continued:

Life is a matter of survival. I'm surrounded by people who don't want me. Through my mind rushes the words of my favorite teacher — "Always continue to walk tall." I tried being strong, but it was not always easy. Life is precarious. No one knows what tomorrow will bring.

In the meantime, we remained in the same apartment surrounded by people who did not want us. Each morning we got dressed, had break- fast, and walked to school. When we returned home, we tidied, prepared dinner, and did our school work. There was hardly any fun in our life.

The highlight of our day was when Herman visited us after dinner. He came to check on us and usually stayed for about an hour.

One day when he came to the apartment, he did not like what he saw. The place was strewn with trash and the dishes piled high in the sink. He realized that we were too young for this type of living arrangement and that it would be better for us to live in some sort of supervised institution, rather than in a small, dusty, and unheated flat with no one to watch over us.

After a few days of walking up and down the streets of Vienna, he finally found us a small orphanage. He told us that it had a nurturing reputation, and he happened to like the headmaster. On his tour of the fa- cility, he found out that the children lived in barracks once used as shelter for soldiers. The following day he brought us there for a tour, but when I walked through its doors, I immediately had bad feelings about the place.

She wrote about her impression of the orphanage:

What had I done to deserve such a life? Every corner just seems crueler than the last. I just don't understand. The next day my sister and I were placed with a group of hundreds of girls, ranging in ages from six to fourteen. The other girls huddled together whispering what I thought were secrets about me. I absolutely refused to associate with them. I found them too childish, plus they didn't understand or even care what Beronia and I had survived, plus the fact that we had no parents and endured the long journey from Poland to live in a very new place. What made it even harder was that I was the oldest girl in the orphanage.

My grandmother continued:

I huddled in a corner with my sister at my side. After breakfast, we were told to line up outside the door. We walked in a line two by two toward a big yard full of trees. The yard was boarded up with a large surrounding wall. I thought I was in prison, yet I had done nothing wrong. At night, I crawled over to my sister's bed, got in, and cried until I had no more tears. We had a long talk and decided not to stay there.

Because I was the older sister, I devised an escape plan. The next morning, when we went for our daily walk, I stepped out of the row of girls, leaving my sister alone. I ran and hid behind a tree. When the students reentered the barracks, I climbed to the top of a tree and found myself sitting high on a metal fence. What I saw turned my blood to ice. On the other side of the fence, extending as far as my eyes could see, was a rather large cemetery. I was so afraid of those ghostly places. As I crawled along the top of the fence, I lost my balance and fell onto the boards of a freshly dug grave. I shivered. I thought I was part of a horror movie. I pulled myself out of the grave and ran in circles searching for an exit. I raced outside not knowing where I was. I ended up on the outskirts of the town. In the near distance, I spotted a trolley at the station. The conductor asked me for the fare. I patted my pockets and they were completely devoid of money. He was about to throw me off when an older passenger got up and offered to pay.

Instead of returning to the orphanage, I waited on the steps of Herman's dwelling until he returned from work. I threw myself at him and wailed to no end. He couldn't get away from me. Realizing that I wouldn't go back to the orphanage, he fed me and put me to sleep. The next day, my brother didn't go to work; he stayed home with me. With gentleness in his voice, he begged me to return to the orphanage. He promised to talk things over with the director. He told me to think about my younger sister and how it would be horrible for her to be in the orphanage without me. Full of fear and anger, I allowed him to escort me back, but my heart felt heavy. He said he had a long talk with the director.

When I reentered the orphanage's large doors, the director walked toward me with open arms. The tall and dark-haired woman with penetrating brown eyes seemed more caring on that day. She wasn't as cold as the day before. It was so nice to feel so welcomed. She offered no reproaches, no punishment. She whispered quiet and kind words into my ear. She asked me to try and stay for a while and said she'd do everything to make me feel better.

After some hesitation, I lowered my head and agreed to stay. The director smiled, took my hand, and brought me back to the other children. When my sister saw me walking, she ran toward me and flung herself into my arms. She held me so tight as if I were her lifeline. I had not seen her smile like that in a long time. This warmed my heart. Wanting to be left alone, we both retreated to the corner. After about fifteen minutes, the director, in a gentler tone, tried coaxing us out of the corner. She tried to get me to speak, but I said that there was nothing else to say. Eventually, I reconciled myself to fate and decided to stay.

CHAPTER 8

Girls School in Vienna

For about two years from 1916–1918, my grandmother and her sister continued to live in the orphanage while attending a newly built high school.

My grandmother wrote:

For the first time, I was enrolled in what was called "a real school" in Vienna. I was very unhappy in the beginning because the other pupils made fun of my strange accent, but as soon as they got to know me, they began liking me and became much friendlier.

By the end of the school year, my grandmother had improved so much in school that she earned a scholarship to a four-year commerce school, Verein Wiener Handels-Akademie Fur Madchen (Association of the Viennese Commercial Academy for Young Women), an exclusive private high school.

❀

She continued:

> *Even though I adapted fairly well to this new school, I felt quite different from the other girls. My grades were higher than anyone else's, and some of the girls were envious. My jealousy ran deeper than the others because they all had families and real homes to return to. For me, that was more important than getting good grades. On the weekends the students had visitors who took them away on shopping trips. Their vacations were spent in the country. Sometimes the class differences made me feel so sad that at night all I could do was to curl up in my bed and cry.*

At this point in her journal she didn't mention her sister, but she does bring her up later.

My grandmother continued:

> *Oh, for my woes of starting this school. I was not the equal of these girls. I felt it painfully. I felt so distant to all their talk. I stayed private and to myself. They brought big lunches to school, whereas I often went hungry. The rationing is so small, and even this little bit does not always reach all of the children. The nurses grab whatever they can; they are also hungry. But there are some girls who don't worry about rations and being hungry. Money buys a lot of things.*
>
> *There were many afternoons when I stayed after school when the other kids either walked home or were picked up by their parents. I used to lie and tell my teacher that I wanted to stay to do my schoolwork. But instead of doing my work, I waited until everyone was gone and then I looked up and down the deserted rows of seats for any leftover lunches. Many times, there was no food left over, and so I had to go back to the orphanage, feeling hungry and tired.*

My grandmother wrote about an incident that happened at school when she was thirteen:

One day in January 1917, a large parcel was delivered to the school containing small packages. Before class, our teacher stood up in front of the room and told us about the food relief packages sent to the school from Holland. She reached into a carton and removed one package. She walked directly to my desk.

She offered me one, but I was too ashamed to take it. I didn't want to be the only girl being offered a package. Even though she knew I was hungry, I felt strange taking it in front of my classmates. I told the teacher that I didn't need it, but I had difficulty reassuring her with a straight and serious face. I badly wanted to snatch it from her hand.

During these postwar times, there were a lot of countries helping out school-aged children. In her book *Too Deep Were Our Roots*, Sonia Wachstein discussed how the school doctor in Vienna examined all the kids and then assigned them to eat American *Anspeisang*, or American food supplements for undernourished children. One of their favorite desserts was rice pudding covered with grated chocolate.

Through their actions, my grandmother didn't think that the other children liked her. She felt that most of the time they were ignoring her and not including her in their conversations. However, she was surprised by one pleasant event:

After six months at that school, the students chose their class delegate for the student government. Who could describe my surprise when they elected me? I stood on the elevated platform wanting to thank them, but I choked on my words. I opened my mouth, but simply couldn't speak. When the class saw me speechless, applause rippled through the auditorium. I was absolutely overwhelmed. For a moment I stood still, not uttering a word. I then bowed and caught a glimpse of my torn leather shoes. I wondered how I could be elected for such an important position with such shoes.

That night I could hardly fall sleep. I promised myself to help my classmates as best I could and whenever possible. I kept my word. Everyone was also very helpful to me. Whenever I had the chance to assist a student with homework, I was generously paid, and this helped me pay for my books and school supplies.

Some students in my grandmother's school went away for the winter months. Some left for weeks on ski tours, some retreated to their mountain homes, and others retreated to the warmer regions of Italy. After the vacation, some students returned to school a few days late holding a doctor's certificate attesting that for health reasons they needed an extended vacation. In spite of being voted class valedictorian, my grandmother still felt extremely jealous and envious of those children.

My grandmother wrote:

There was nobody to take me away. Anywhere. For anything, not even my brother Herman. He was welcoming at first, but that didn't last long.

It seemed as if once they were settled in the orphanage, Herman distanced himself from the girls. In her journal my grandmother made no mention of him taking either my grandmother or her sister out of the orphanage, even for one day. I imagine that his attitude was greatly influenced by his wife, Lilly.

My mother used to visit her Aunt Lilly during her annual trips to Vienna in the 1970s and 1980s. She said that she was the type of woman who was jealous if anyone even spoke to her husband. Lilly only became friendly to us after Herman passed away, sometime in the 1970s. Once she visited us at our house in New York. I remember her as a short and skinny woman with dark brown hair, wearing a brown business suit with stiff brown shoes to match. She had sunken brown eyes that were difficult to make eye contact with. She spoke little English and admitted to hating Americans. My mother interpreted for both of us. I remember her penetrating stare and how she repeatedly told my mother how beautiful I was, as if that was all that mattered.

Lilly brought me a white enamel bracelet with purple flowers, which at the time I thought was so ugly. Of course, sixteen-year-olds rarely express approval of anything bought by adults. I think that bracelet is still tucked away in some heirloom box in my closet as a souvenir of my Austrian heritage.

CHAPTER 9

Becoming A Woman

In 1919, at the end of my grandmother's first year at the high school, the students received report cards. Their work was graded as poor, good, and excellent. She received an "excellent" grade in all her subjects, including German, French Correspondence, English Correspondence, Commerce, History, Geometry, Algebra, Political Arithmetic, Business Arithmetic, Natural History, Physics, Chemistry, Business Correspondence, Stenography, and Penmanship.

After receiving her report card, my grandmother wrote:

I was so surprised to have done so well in my studies. I was awarded "Highest Honors," and eventually graduated with a "Certificate of Maturity with Excellence." In those days this was a rare acknowledgment, and I was so proud of myself.

Translated from the German language.

WIENER HANDELSAKADEMIE FUER MAEDCHEN
Public Institutional Right according to stipulation of the Federal Depart-
ment of Interior and Education dated June 16, 1921, Z.10373/11-5
II., HOLLANDSTRASSE 4.

Z. 21.   CERTIFICATE OF MATURITY.

Rebekka Reinharz,
born May 22, 1903, in Kalusz, in Galicia, mos. religion, after completion
of a 2-years-course of School of Commerce, has attended the

Wiener Handelsakademie fuer Maedchen

from school year 1919/20 till end of school year 1922/23 and has submitted
at summer term 1923 to examination of maturity, according to rules and
regulations dated March 18, 1920, B.A. No. 35, with the following
results in the single courses of study:

German Language	100 %
French Language and Commercial Correspondence	100 %
English Language and Commercial Correspondence	100 %
Geography of Commerce and Trade	100 %
General and Commercial History	100%
Mathematics (Algebra and Political Arithmetics)	90 %
Commercial Arithmetics	90 %
Practice Comptoir (Study of Commerce, Commercial-" (Correspondence and Bookkeeping)	100 %
Study of Merchandise and Mechanical Technology	100 %
Law of Commerce, Law of Bill-of-Exchange and Trade Law	100 %
National Economics	100 %

The conduct during the attendance of the Handelsakademie
was   100 %
On the basis of this examen the above-mentioned was
accorded the
CERTIFICATE of MATURITY with EXCELLENCE.
(Highest Honors)
Vienna, June 25, 1923.

signed:Franz Doerfel
Predident of the examinati on Commission

Dr.Olga Ehrenhaft-Steindler   Dr. Benedict Fendrich
Government Director   Class Headmaster

This is to vertify that the above ist the true translation of the German original.

Dr. Wilhelm Schaag, Director.

Regina's graduation certificate

As soon as I returned to the orphanage, I immediately ran to phone Herman to share the wonderful news. With some reluctance in his voice, he said he'd drive to the orphanage that evening and give me a hug. I was really surprised at even his slight display of affection. The director of the orphanage acted like she cared about my good report card, but was too busy, and distractedly congratulated me. The following day was the last day of school and the principal, a middle-aged man with a mustache, called me into his office.

"Regina," he said, pointing to the chair in front of his desk, "Have a seat."

I wondered what I might have done wrong, and through my mind flashed a number of events of the past few days.

"I can't tell you how proud I am of you," he finally said. Suddenly I felt all the muscles in my body become limp. It was not very often that I received such compliments.

"This is the first time in the school's history that a student has been given the status of 'praiseworthy.' This is remarkable, and you should be proud of yourself. Really proud," he said.

I thanked him and then sat frozen in my chair. I wanted him to say more. I was like a hungry stray cat craving nourishment. After a few minutes of small talk, he wished me a good day. I walked down the corridor leading to the outdoors. On the steps outside the building, I propped myself against the wall and unrolled my certificate. A tear fell on its black ink, making it run slightly. I pulled out a pink handkerchief from my pocket and dabbed the certificate.

I looked across the large field in front of the school and reflected on the day two years earlier when I ran through a similar-looking field searching for my mother. Even though I knew she didn't love me, at that moment I would have done almost anything in the world to have her standing beside me. I needed to make someone else proud, anyone. As I *stood on the school's steps, streams of girls ran happily past me into the arms of their parents. Some began unrolling their certificates as they ran, anxiously presenting them to their parents.*

My grandmother continued:

The front of the school exploded with kissing, rejoicing, and many consoling words. But nobody waited for me. I returned to the dormitory that was now full of chaos with children packing their bags for summer vacation. Everyone seemed happy, but for me the air was bleak. Although the temperature was warm, my insides felt like icicles. I had no one with whom to share my certificate. I walked slowly into the dining room holding the certificate tightly in my hand. The chairs were stacked on top of the tables. A sad emptiness filled the room. After a few moments, I folded it up and put it away in a book.

Most of the students left the hot city and went straight to the mountains. Each day during the summer, I walked to the park beside the orphanage. When I came back, I ran to the calendar and counted the days until school started. The summer seemed as if it would never end.

I was so happy on the first day of school. The students flocked together in the classroom wearing new outfits and new shoes. This made me sad. I had on all old clothes. They were holding stacks of books and sharing stories about their vacation away. They all hated returning to school, but not me. I was so glad to be back.

On the first day of school I was happy to have one dress without rips or holes. I wore the same dress every day and shuddered at the thought of what might happen if it entered a new stage of being: beyond repair. The boys certainly did not look in my direction. They looked at the girls wearing pretty clothes and different ones every day, and those who were from good homes. That's who they looked at. My teacher told me that my beauty far surpassed any clothes or families. She encouraged me to just be myself, and in the end, everything would work itself out.

My grandmother wrote this about the latter part of 1919:

> *In October 1919, a few months after I turned sixteen, I began hunting for an after-school job. Each morning I woke up, washed, and got dressed for school. It was starting to get cold, and so on some days I had to slip on my winter coat. Each day on the way to school I had this habit of stopping off at the corner store for the morning newspaper. Just like some of the older gentlemen, I sat down on the bench outside the store and read the paper. I read the job section for a bank job.*
>
> *One Friday afternoon on the way home from school and after one week of reading the newspapers, I spotted an advertisement on the circular display board outside a bank on the main street. It said that if anyone was interested in a bank job, they should appear on Monday morning for an interview. No job requirements were listed.*
>
> *In anticipation of the interview, I didn't sleep all weekend. On Monday morning after the alarm rang, I thought about what my favorite schoolteacher told me about how important school was. I decided that since my sister was younger, I'd send her to the bank with a letter I'd prepared for the bank manager. This is what it said:*

> *Dear Mr. Stern:*
>
> *I cannot miss school today. Please understand. Please give my sister the job application. I will complete it and then shall stop in to see you immediately after school.*
>
> *Sincerely,*
> *Regina Klein*

After school my grandmother wrote:

I arrived at the entrance to the bank at exactly three o'clock. I asked the receptionist near the front door if I could speak to the bank manager. I was frightened at my own audacity and gumption. I didn't know how in the world I'd get the job.

During my research about Vienna at that time, I learned students were placed either on an academic or business track. My grandmother decided to follow the academic track, although nowhere in her journal did she discuss that decision and why she chose it. I suspect it might have been because of her apparent interest in medicine. Because of her decision to follow the academic track, she had learned only a small amount of shorthand and even less typing. I think that she thought it might have hindered her from getting a bank job, but it was something that she wanted to try anyway.

My grandmother continued:

After my very short interview with the bank manager and after looking me up and down a few times, he said that he wanted to hire me for the job.

Here's what he told me: "I want you to begin tomorrow, but I do have some concerns. I wonder how you'll have time to do what other teenagers do, like going to the movies or meeting with friends at cafes, if you work every day immediately following school and until the early evening hours."

I wanted to cry. I was so touched by his concern for me, but I told him I did not like the movies, and furthermore, meeting with friends did not really interest me.

My grandmother wrote this the following day:

At the end of the next school day, I gathered my schoolbooks and rushed to the front door of the bank. I adjusted my skirt and fixed my hair by looking into the bank's window. I smiled at my image and pulled back my shoulders. Once inside, I asked the lady sitting behind the small reception desk for Mr. Stern, the friendly gentleman who had interviewed me the day before.

To my dismay, my second impression of the bank was not the same as the first one. I looked around and everything seemed stuffy, dusty, and messy. The employees rushed about not taking any notice of me. Files were piled up high on the cabinets, and more were stacked on the floor. The desks were cluttered with papers.

An older woman with her gray hair in a bun approached me and said, "Hello, I'm Mrs. Lunz, your boss." She looked me up and down as if I were a piece of meat. She outwardly displayed some dissatisfaction at what she saw. I was really disappointed about not being greeted by Mr. Stern. The woman walked me to a room and told me that's where I should leave my school bag. While placing it in the cabinet, Mrs. Lunz's dark brown eyes focused on its worn-out condition. She did a soldier's about-face and brought me to my new desk.

"These papers, here," she said, pointing to a stack on the desk, "need to be filed as soon as possible. You can begin now and I'll check on you in a few minutes."

I glanced around trying to acquaint myself with the surroundings. I flipped through the papers and pulled out the top filing cabinet drawer, fumbling through its contents trying to figure out what went where. Unlike others working at the bank, Mrs. Lunz showed little enthusiasm in either me or the work I was appointed to do.

During my first week I really went out of my way to impress Mrs.

Lunz, but the woman managed to find fault with everything I did. She'd say things like, "Didn't I tell you how to do that?" or "You did that wrong," rarely complimenting me on all the good things I did. As time went on, Mrs. Lunz seemed disenchanted with everything about me. Apparently, I was not very good at making women happy.

"You work much too quickly. You must spread your work out during your hours here," she told me once when I asked for more work to do. It seemed as if she was bothered by my actual presence at the bank.

My grandmother shared some of her concerns:

When I came to Mrs. Lunz, she made hurtful comments about my clothes, saying they shouldn't have stains or be ripped. I told her I didn't have the money for new things and that's why I was working. She was not sympathetic to my feelings, and many days after work I ran home crying. I hated that woman. Her ways reminded me of my mother's. She haunted me — all those painful and hurtful words.

Finally, I decided that since I had enough money saved up, I'd enroll in a dance course on Saturday evenings. I really needed something to distract me from my daily woes. Plus, learning how to dance had been a dream of mine for a very long time. During the evenings, as a young girl in Galicia, I used to peek in the windows of dance halls. I stared at all the men and women dressed up in fancy clothes. I loved watching them dance around the large mirrored room with wooden floors. With no hesitancy in their stride, the couples glided across the dance floor, looking as if they were floating among the clouds. I liked the carefree sensibilities of dancing and the way the women's skirts twirled when they were swung around by the men. I admired how the men held the women around their waists. Happiness and joy seemed to fill the room.

She continued:

With the money I earned at the bank, I badly wanted to buy a new outfit and high-heeled dancing shoes. The following Saturday evening, I arrived at the dance hall eager to find a boy to dance with. I was already sixteen and had many dreams about being held by a boy. During the first few sessions, the boys did not show any interest in me. No one stood up to ask me to dance. I sat in the corner watching the others. Once, this homely and shy boy, looking as if he missed his mother, came to ask me to dance. He hardly knew how to hold me or where to put his feet on the dance floor. After a few moments, I told him I was tired and had to go home.

After a few weeks I saved up even more money to buy another party dress. It was white with red ribbing framing my tiny waist and wrists. I put on matching red lipstick. I was quite proud of my looks and returned Saturday night to the dance hall. When I was not asked to dance, my confidence waned again. For one more night I ended up sitting in the corner by myself — not one boy approached me.

I looked like a forsaken soul. In school, I participated in class and shared my knowledge with everyone. In many ways I knew more than the others, but at this dance hall, I felt as if I was on slippery ground, although in so many ways, it provided me with a sense of intrigue.

She wrote this about dance class:

In dance class, when the first boy asked me to dance, I questioned him outright why no one else asked me to dance. He told me I was too serious and never laughed; boys didn't think they'd have fun with me. From that day on, I paid close attention to my actions. I tried hard to please my partners during dancing lessons and somehow learned how to engage in small talk.

She wrote this in the spring of 1920 when she was seventeen years old:

I find so much peace in visiting the city parks near my school. Each day I find a quiet spot on a bench outside and pull out my schoolwork from my bag. The dormitory was much too noisy, disturbing, and gloomy. Before long, the school year ended again, and I was faced with the loneliness inherent to all of my summers. I had hoped this summer vacation would be different. A friend of my mother's invited me to spend time at her country home, just north of Vienna. Ecstatic about taking a train trip, I accepted the invitation and immediately bought my train ticket.

The train pulled into the station closest to my dormitory. I stood there with my small leather suitcase, the one looking as if it had survived multiple wars. When the train came to a halt, I glanced inside its clear windows. It was packed with students talking and seemingly excited about their summer vacation. I was first in line and climbed the stairs of the passenger car and almost immediately found an empty seat beside a large window. At the next stop, a young man wearing a beret and holding a small suitcase boarded. I watched him maneuver up the aisle in my direction. Surprisingly, he sat down in the vacant seat beside me. He looked older than me. He was dressed as a businessman with trousers, suspenders, and shiny leather shoes. When he took off his beret, I noticed his slicked-back black hair. His smile exposed two shallow dimples. I thought he was really good-looking.

We ended up speaking for a while, and I learned that his name was Zygo and he was on his way home to visit his parents. We sat together for the entire two-day train trip. When I announced that I would be getting off at the next stop, he leaned over and asked for my address. We agreed to meet at the end of the summer when we both returned to Vienna.

My grandmother wrote about her arrival in the country:

When I arrived at the country house, for the first time in my life it felt like home. I didn't have to answer to anyone. It wasn't like being in the dormitory, where if I didn't get up when the bell rang, the supervisor entered the picture and I'd get into a lot of trouble.

I woke up when I wanted and enjoyed endless hours of swimming in the nearby stream. Unlike boarding school, the kitchen did not close if I arrived a few minutes late for breakfast. When I was hungry, I wandered unquestioned down to the kitchen for something to eat. For me, this was a dream come true. During those two months of vacation, I filled the hollows of my body and became a lot taller.

She wrote this at the end of the summer:

When summer vacation was over, I returned to Vienna for my last year of high school. The year went very quickly because of my relationship with Zygo. We met a few times each week in nearby cafés.

At first we met to talk about school. But soon our meetings became the pretext for something more emotional, more meaningful. We discovered that we were both lonely and lonesome, and for this reason needed to be together.

I learned that Zygo lived by himself. Sometimes he invited me up to his apartment and other times we sat talking in restaurants near my dormitory. For hours we discussed everything from families to politics. We both enjoyed people-watching, and Zygo told me that one day he wanted to be a writer. Sometimes we sat so long in one café that we would get dirty looks from the owner. I wanted to be with Zygo all of the time. It upset me how he was not allowed to visit me at my school. I was allowed to go out with him, but I had to check in by ten o'clock in the evening if I didn't want to get into trouble.

Zygo often told me how pretty I was and how different I seemed from the other girls. He said he loved me very much. I felt so awkward accepting his kind and generous words. At times I was wary of Zygo, yet at other times I gravitated to his attention. For the most part, whenever I had spare time between work and school, especially on Sundays, I dashed across town to meet him. It did not take long for us to become inseparable.

He told me when he finished his studies he wanted to marry me. He said he didn't want to consider anyone else in his life, just me. But he warned me it would take him about five years to complete his studies. He said that he hoped I would be patient and wait for him.

After one year of dating, my grandmother wrote this:

As luck would have it, just before we were to celebrate the first anniversary of our acquaintance, we began fighting. Zygo was getting busier with his studies, and when he wasn't studying, he focused his time on finding a job to pay for his food and rent. His parents were poor farmers and were unable to help him.

The quarrels between us became more and more intense. First they were caused by small issues like where to have dinner, but soon the topics of disagreement spanned even larger philosophical issues.

One day when I was on my way home from my bank job, I happened to spot Zygo in a café. I looked closer and realized that he was sitting with another woman who I'd never seen before. I was sure it was him. His back was toward the street I was walking down, but I could easily identify Zygo's slightly balding head, inherited, he claimed, from his mother's side of the family. The woman facing him appeared a few years older than me, and there was something hauntingly familiar about her, but I wasn't sure where I had seen her.

I was tempted to stop and say hello, but I decided to keep on walking past them, as they were seemingly enthralled in their conversation, which appeared to be more than casual but less than professional. The woman was giggling, and I noticed flirtatious glances being exchanged between the two. The woman smiled as if Zygo just paid her a compliment, something he had frequently done to me. I had become easily addicted to his comments.

At that moment I thought about one of our last conversations where he spoke about this woman, named Ingrid, saying they had remained good friends. In my mind, there was a safe distance between friends, yet that line is crossed only when they became lovers. With my intuitive sense, which my mother used to tell me I had, I felt as if Zygo was cheating on me and having a clandestine relationship with this woman. We had just spoken that morning, and he never mentioned anything about having coffee with her.

For the first time in my life, I had given my soul to another person and embarked on the virtue of trust. I badly wanted to believe that he loved me, but something told me that our relationship was doomed. And once again, now at the age of eighteen, I felt terribly lonely and had feelings of abandonment. Instead of making a scene, I returned to my dormitory.

That night Zygo phoned to see how my week went. I answered the phone tersely, and said that everything was fine. Here's how our conversation went:

"You don't sound like yourself," he said.

"I don't?"

"No. What's wrong?"

"Nothing."

"Come on, Regina, I know something is bothering you."

"What do you think?" I asked.

"How am I to know? I haven't seen you in a couple of days."

I thought the line went dead. Silence prevailed.

"I saw you with that girl," I said.

"Where'd you see me?" he innocently asked.

"At the Paris coffeehouse."

Silence continued and then he intercepted.

"Yes. Ingrid and I were having a cup of coffee. It had been planned for a long time. Did that bother you?"

"Coffee doesn't bother me, but I got a sense that it was more than that. Zygo, tell me. Do you want me to disappear from your life? I will if that's what you want."

"Regina, what a silly question! Of course I don't want you to disappear."

"Well, is it possible to love two women?"

"No. Never. Ingrid and I are just friends. You knew that."

"Yes. I knew that, but the question is whether I believe that."

"Trust me, Regina. Please."

"Listen. I don't want to talk now. I'm busy, plus quite upset," I said, and hung up.

The following day was my birthday, and Zygo visited with a bouquet of flowers. They made an exception and allowed him in because it was my birthday.

"That's nice," I said, "but you never bought me flowers before. Are you sorry about something?"

"Listen, Regina, stop being so suspicious. Nothing happened between Ingrid and me. We're just friends."

"Time will tell," I said, feeling so much pain in my heart. I really *loved Zygo. I loved everything about him — his looks, his intelligence, his charm. I was happy to have found someone to grasp onto emotionally. Zygo provided relief from the ghosts of my tormented past, but I had been misled and was forced to face the world alone, again. I wondered if that was my destiny.*

In 1921, at the age of eighteen, my grandmother felt lonelier than ever. She no longer had Zygo's companionship to ground her and give her the love she craved. She decided it was better to walk away from him before he walked away from her.

My grandmother wrote:

The situation around me was dreadful. It was a pity I had survived and was still alive. I looked around and the unemployment rate in Vienna soared, because the Viennese had just lost the war. Everyone was warned about the dismal state of the Austrian economy. A few days after my high school graduation, I began hunting for another bank job. I enjoyed the banking world and had already accumulated some experience there.

In her journal, my grandmother never mentioned what happened to her first bank job.

She continued:

From early in the morning until the end of the workday, I walked up and down the streets of the financial district of Vienna where banks were lined up one after another. Restlessly, I trekked from one building to the next trying to convince each manager to spend just a few moments speak-

ing with me. Most of them smiled, opening the door for me and then sent me on my way. On a few rare occasions, I actually had the opportunity to say a word or two to the personnel manager.

She wrote:

I tramped and tramped up and down the stairs of the bank buildings. It was near closing time when I entered this small bank. The doorman asked me many questions, to which I cautiously shook my head and said "Yes." Finally, I stood before the mighty personnel manager. He took the diploma from my hand and glanced at it. Distracted, he listened to my talk. I desperately tried to impress upon him how badly I needed the work. I implored him. I begged him to give me any kind of job at his bank. I told him I am a quick learner and am willing to be trained in whatever area I would be needed. But, he said half to himself and half to me, if he could use anybody at all, it would be a male, not a female. Their policy, in the past, had been to hire only male employees.

After hearing this, I stretched up high onto my toes, looked into his dead brown eyes, and begged him to believe that I'd do a better job than any man and would work for less pay. He stopped and said that he would have to think about it and he'd let me know. I begged him not to give me false hopes and to let me know right away. His eyes moved to the door as his hand pulled it open.

I spent a morose evening waiting for the arrival of the next morning's mail. I thought it would be a good idea to continue my job hunt and not to set my expectations too high. I got dressed in my best clothes and set out on the hunt once again. Just after locking my apartment door and heading down the stairs to the street, I came face to face with the mailman. He handed me three letters. I sat on the stairs and flipped through them. I jumped and nearly fell down the stairs. There was a letter from the *personnel manager at the bank. He asked me to come to work. I could not contain my excitement. I went dancing in the streets.*

This story about my grandmother's surprise at being hired by the bank resonates with a story in my own life. After obtaining my nursing license, I was hired as a cardiovascular nurse in a postoperative unit in a local teaching hospital. I nursed patients who had various types of open heart surgeries. Part of my job involved dealing with many emotional issues, because many of the surgical patients were men in high-powered executive positions and were not the most obliging patients.

In a short period of time, I mastered my job and was promoted to team captain. This involved making the weekly schedules and going on rounds with the doctors each morning and reporting the patients' status. Although I worked as a full-time nurse, when home, I researched and wrote health articles for national publications. Deep inside of me lurked a certain discontent and lack of challenge as a bedside nurse.

After one year of bedside nursing, my father came to visit us in our home in Montreal. My dad was the manager of a retail chain in Brooklyn, and I knew that I'd inherited his administrative and organizational acumen.

I shared with him my discontent with my job.

"Why don't you look for something else? It's silly to be locked into a job. You're still young and don't yet have a family. It would be different for someone like me with a family to support."

On Sunday morning during breakfast, he suggested we pull out the classified section of our local newspaper to check out what nursing positions were available. One particular ad caught my eye. "Immediate Opening. Director of Nursing position in a 125-bed chronic care hospital. Flexible salary. Call (514) 842-1567."

What appealed to me about this ad was that they didn't ask for experience.

"Call," my father urged me, "You just never know."

"How could I be hired as a director of nursing? I've only practiced nursing for a year."

"You can do it. Just try."

My father's confidence in me was overwhelming. I made the phone call, and the personnel director set up an interview for that afternoon at three o'clock.

During the interview, my father sat in the car reading the remainder of the newspaper. An hour later I came out and told him that I had been hired for the job and was to begin the following Monday. He pulled me close to him and gave me a tight hug.

"I knew it. I knew it!" he said. "I'm so proud of you."

I felt like dancing around my father's car like my grandmother danced in the streets when she got her bank job.

∝

CHAPTER 10

Regina and Samuel

Except for one incident, the time period between 1922 and 1926 is poorly documented in my grandmother's journal. I do know that she graduated from high school and worked in an Austrian bank from 1923 to 1924. She had received a powerful letter of recommendation from her boss at that bank. In some documents recovered after finding her journal, I learned that during this period she was also accepted into medical school in Vienna. She actually began the program and for two years was a full-time student, until she ran out of money and then eventually got married. My grandfather did not encourage her to continue the program, although it had always been her life's dream to be a doctor.

My grandmother, now twenty-three years old, wrote:

> One cold day in January 1927, I visited a local tailor shop in search of a new winter coat. Hans' Coats was a reasonably priced garment

store situated on a small side street off the main boulevard. Hans was best known for his custom-made winter coats. The store's windows featured coat samples hanging on mannequins of varying sizes. The set of bells strung above the store's door signaled a customer's arrival. Mannequins wearing half-finished winter coats lined the sides of the store. The coats were held together at the seams by pins and white basting stitches.

Exposing a gold-capped-tooth smile, a suited gentleman with a measuring tape slung around his neck greeted me at the door. Here is how our interaction went:

"Hello, Miss," he said, speaking in a soft German. "May I help you?"

"My winter coat is falling apart. Can you help me find a new one?" I said, turning both hole-ridden pockets inside out.

"With pleasure," he said, motioning me to the rear of the store where the less expensive coats hung sparsely on the racks.

I stood in front of a rack of black coats. I glanced at the man, and his expression intrigued me. There was something warm and familiar about him, as if I'd seen him somewhere before. Being in his company, I felt completely comfortable. He stared at me as if a question dangled from his lips. After trying on a selection of coats, I held up a black one with a brown fur collar.

"That's a good choice," he said, smiling and repeatedly moving his shoulders forward as if he had a tic.

I spun myself around in front of the three-way mirror revealing the coat's angles. "How much is this one?"

"For you," he hesitated, "I'll give you a good price. How does two schillings sound?"

I pulled out my little brown change purse with the push metal closure. I had exactly two schillings.

Delighted about making my first big purchase with money that I had earned from my bank job, I removed the bills, holding them tightly in *my hand. He signaled for me to sit in the chair opposite him at the desk. From his drawer, he pulled out a receipt pad and a pen. He placed the pen on the pad and leaned over the desk toward me.*

"Miss, may I ask you something?" His shoulders pushed forward again.

"Yes," I said, fumbling for a handkerchief in my purse.

"You see, I have this store here, but I also have another one on the other side of town. That's where I usually work. My wife, she runs this store, but today she had to go visit her mother — poor woman is sick; they think she has sugar [diabetes]. You see, I also manage a modeling agency. And well, I'm always looking for attractive young ladies. Young ladies like you."

For a moment, I glanced around the store to ascertain my safety on this Viennese back street. My intuitive judgment of character had never deceived me; I thought he was a good person.

He continued, "I wonder if you'd be interested in doing some modeling for us? They're very nice clothes — young looking." He pulled out a photo album from the drawer.

"Does it pay?"

"Absolutely, but it depends upon your experience."

"I have none."

"Don't worry about that part; just let me know if you'd be interested." With arms crossed, he sat back in his chair. I noticed his initials embroidered on the wrist of his shirt.

"Listen, why don't you go home and think about it. How about you call me tomorrow after school?"

"I'll do that. Thanks," I said, standing up.

"Now there's no rush," he added. "But it would just be wonderful if you could join us for next week's class. We're beginning a new session."

My grandmother continued writing about that modeling job:

For the next few months, I worked at the bank and then took the twenty-minute trolley ride to Mr. Oslo's evening model training class. On the evening of the second session, a tall blond man about my age, in his early twenties, walked confidently to the rear of the store toward the training room. He had broad shoulders and good posture. His smooth complexion and well-contoured face immediately captivated my attention. I had this soft spot for men wearing dark suits, and his was a thin, navy blue pinstripe. He wore a white shirt and a red polka-dot tie with a matching handkerchief, fluffed in a special way in his jacket pocket. Our eyes linked and he cracked a smile, accentuating his dimples. I had never seen a man with such naturally light blond hair.

I immediately pulled my shoulders back. My mother's words echoed in my mind: "Always stand tall, no matter what." I really felt my mother's pointer finger running down my spine reminding me to stand up straight.

During class that day, I learned that he was the only male model working for Mr. Oslo and was coincidentally the best model in the city. As a matter of fact, he was not a student like me; he was the one who demonstrated what the teacher wanted to show the other students.

That man was Samuel, who would one day become my grandfather. Regina and Samuel dated for a short time before Samuel asked for her hand in marriage. On April 10, 1927, Rabbi Josef Bach married them in Vienna.

My mother says that for as long as she remembers, my grandparents had a rocky marriage. "Your grandmother married for security, and not for love," she said. She grasped onto the first man who expressed any sort of

Regina and Samuel's marriage certificate

love and promised to take care of her. But unfortunately, my grandparents were both strong-willed and ended up fighting about everything. After a few years, they thought a baby would draw them closer and give them someone else's needs to focus on.

My grandmother wrote this about her first and only baby, my mother:

On August 12, 1930, Eva Marcelle was born in a small hospital on the outskirts of Vienna. When she grew up, she learned that on the day she was born, her father, my husband, Samuel, instead of being at the hospital awaiting his new baby's arrival, sat in a Viennese café sipping coffee and nibbling gugelhupf, [a Viennese yeast cake with almonds and raisins baked in a special bundt pan]. Even after Eva was born, Sam was either working or hanging around Viennese cafés. I received little emotional support from him, something I really lacked in the early stages of our marriage.

My grandmother was a lady of leisure who played bridge and enjoyed social dancing. She also spent a great deal of time studying and, along with their maid, Mizi, attending to Eva. During those times in Vienna, nearly all middle-class families had the luxury of having a maid.

According to Sonia Wachstein, in *Too Deep Were Our Roots*, many of the maids were peasant girls who could not stay on the small farms and came to the city, their education finished after eight years of school. Some had illegitimate children that they left behind. They were often hired for very low wages, learning the necessary skills on the job, and their lives were utterly miserable. Maids sometimes had a tiny room behind the kitchen. In smaller apartments, they slept in the kitchen.

Regina and Diana's mother, Eva, 1930

CHAPTER 11

The Nazis Take Vienna

My grandmother's journal made little mention of the years 1930–1938. I can only deduce that during those years, my grandparents were busy raising Eva. From an early age, Eva was taken for hiking trips to the Vienna Woods, which was a common outing for Austrians. My mother said, "There was not one person living in Vienna who did not go to the Vienna Woods." After breakfast, on days when she was not playing bridge, Regina would prepare a backpack with lunch and they would spend the day hiking.

Austria has long been considered a hiking-crazed country, and its capital had a network of easy-to-reach city trails. Regina and Eva hiked through green spaces and then meandered into the leafy parts of the Vienna Woods or set their eyes on the city's vineyards. Along the way there were places to eat where the adults might have a coffee and cake or a beer for a burst of energy. Sometimes on their longer walks they would wander around to the giant Ferris wheel at the famous Prater Park.

Among my grandmother's papers I found a loose document typewritten by her in English in 1938 where she recounted a discussion of mundane domestic events, all in the context of the confusion surrounding the sudden Nazi invasion:

How strange is our life? We live for today, plan for tomorrow after a certain pattern of the yesterday, and then, out of the blue sky, another day is born that changes our entire life so very thoroughly that never again will it be the same.

Today, I got up at about eleven o'clock feeling rather listless. I was out late the night before. The maid put my breakfast on my night table, and as usual it got cold, stale, and untouched. Once again it went back to the kitchen. The child, my only, is in the second grade. She gets to school without my help, assisted by our maid, Mizi. I hurry to do a little shopping before she comes home for lunch.

There I stand waiting for her and feeling guilty. Eva had to get up so early in the morning while I was fast asleep. She has to do her schoolwork, liking it or not, but I will not force myself to do anything. Somehow, I will do something unabsorbing, yet pleasant, to make the day go by. The school bell rings and the children storm out and here is my Eva storming down the steps and out into the streets of Vienna. I am animated and happy. She is a darling. Her little nose got red from the cold, and she told me about the happenings in school and the teacher who does not like her because she can't keep a straight line while writing. True, straight lines cause us a lot of chagrin, but then I console myself by thinking how should such a little child be able to keep a straight line on unlined paper? Why not give just lined paper and stop troubling them? Well, it must be some

German precision that they try to implant into my child. She comes home, has lunch, and then she naps, while I lie down with a book or newspaper.

In the mid-to late 1930s, the political climate in Austria began changing rapidly. Beginning in March 1938, German troops seized Austria. Hitler was cheered when he arrived in Vienna to announce the *Anschluss* (union) of Austria and Germany. As a result, Austria's fate became tied to Germany's, whose quest for power led to the beginning of World War II.

She continued:

> *The more I read the less I understand. They speak about the Nazi formations and their party and all those speeches. I can't read a column to its end. The newspaper embodies and mirrors our daily lives. I force myself to continue reading, but do not finish. For years there were suspicions of Hitler taking over. Well, I believe somehow that things will not be the same a year from now. I would rather read my book to get away from those unpleasant thoughts.*

> *It is four in the afternoon. Eva is sleeping. I am getting ready for a bridge party. I dress carefully and consult the mirror and again see the same thing as last time. Surely, I am rather good looking and well dressed and most certainly very soigné. I will go now and amuse myself just like I do each and every day. What else could I do at home by myself all day long? My husband leaves early each morning to look after his business and does not come home all day. I am alone all day long. I am lonely inside and out. In the evenings he sometimes calls to tell me he will wait for me in the café or some restaurant. But those ideas are very vague and*

uncertain. Sometimes he doesn't want to go out at all. I feel let down and lonesome. I am then tempted to reproach him and start a series of quarrels and tell him the "truth." But then I realize that life is too short and it is not worth it.

For ten years this has been the pattern of my life. I knew things would never change just by "talking things over." How different life turns out to be from what you imagined it would be. I thought I would share the life of my husband, and mine too would be shared. But no, all is well divided: he brings home the money and I manage the household. On the rare occasions when we are together, I listen to his business talk, but he is rather impatient with my talk about managing things at home. Outrageous! What would he do with a wife who talks pots and meals and gossip all day?

I do none of these things. I do not talk about pots and pans, and neither do I cook in them. I do not gossip, as I have only a few good friends and we don't share cheap talk. But still he is rather impatient listening to me — probably because we are married. The prophet never amounts to much in his own country. Maybe I am too serious-minded. I often wonder why I couldn't have as carefree a life as Mrs. Miller [neighbor] or any other woman of my class? I am married, therefore I can do whatever I want and not be bothered with my reputation. I have enough money for the small pleasures of life and more time to do whatever I please. No woman of my class has worked, and the least of her worries are to spend her time profitably. I had enough misery as a child — now I live for my bridge games.

"Mizi," I say, "Take good care of Eva and do not leave her alone for a minute and I will call you when I am under way and inquire how she is." Mizi continued to assure me what she shall do with the child and what she shall not. She knows all my warnings by heart. Repetition is the mother of *knowledge, they say, and so I repeat all my wishes regarding the child every day anew.*

Despite the rise of the Austrian Nazi Party, my grandmother wrote about an incident with her husband:

One day we sat in a neighborhood café. I couldn't believe that Sam told me that he'd rather die in Vienna than move anywhere else in the world. I put down my porcelain cup and stared back at him. With the far-away look you get when looking at something too long, my husband's face turned into my father's. I remembered when he refused to leave Galicia, and now my own husband is showing the same sort of stubbornness. Never had I thought that so many years later I'd be in a similar dilemma. Once again I was faced with the choice of staying or fleeing. I pleaded with Sam to leave, as my own mother had pleaded with my father. Our fate was to be decided some days later.

On November 9, 1938, the Nazis unleashed a wave of pogroms against German Jews. Within a few hours, thousands of synagogues and Jewish businesses and homes were destroyed. The event became known as *Kristall-nacht* (Night of Broken Glass), for the shattered glass lining the streets. Similar events were occurring in Austria.

In her journal, my grandmother recounted a horrific event that occurred on November 12, 1938:

At the time, my husband worked at his brother-in-law, Herman's men's clothing store. He wasn't working on that day and had just left our apartment to do a few errands. He was gone for about half an hour, and during that time three secret service officers holding guns barged into our apartment. I was in the kitchen preparing lunch for me and Eva, who was eight at the time. I turned around and stood at attention. This is how the interaction went:

"Your name?" one asked.

"Regina Reinharz Klein."

"Your religion?"

"Jewish," I said, proudly, but only then did I realize the mistake in my answer.

"You're under arrest," the other officer said.

"What did I do?"

No one answered.

I began yelling, "I have a child here. My husband stepped out to the bank. What will happen?"

"That's not our problem," the third one responded.

"I didn't do anything," I repeated.

I screamed at the top of my lungs as I pulled Eva to me while trying to head for the front door. The men rushed toward us and pushed me against the granite furnace in the corner of the kitchen. One officer then handcuffed me and the other three pushed me out the front door, as I dragged Eva behind.

I was thrown so hard against that furnace that my back got injured. Eva and I remained in jail for a week, and when we were released, I paid a visit to my doctor, who reported that my kidneys were severely bruised. Since that day, I've had recurrent kidney infections. Sometimes the pain is so bad that the doctors think they might have to remove a kidney.

When I finally was released from jail, I realized that the officers had confiscated all of my identification. This became a huge problem once we began the process of immigration.

Soon after *Kristallnacht*, the Viennese Jews began talking about fleeing Vienna. My grandfather was no longer resistant. My grandmother, grandfather, and mother finally decided to pack their suitcases and embark on the next train to Paris, but unfortunately they still did not have proper identification.

CHAPTER 12

Paris to New York

By the end of 1938, my grandmother, grandfather and mother arrived in Paris. My grandmother wrote this about their arrival in Paris:

> *With instructions written on a small piece of paper, Samuel, Eva, and I arrived at the train station in Paris. A short time later, we landed at the home of Rusza and Schrulek, my husband's only surviving sister and her husband.*

My grandmother wrote very little about her stay in Paris. Under cramped conditions in their small city apartment, the five of them lived together for about a year.

During that year, the Germans continued their rout of Europe. In September 1939, after more than twenty-one years of peace, Europe was again at war. With lightning speed and terrifying effectiveness, the Nazis invaded

Poland in what was to become known as the Blitzkrieg. The French and German governments immediately issued an ultimatum to the Third Reich to suspend its aggression. As the Nazis surrounded Warsaw, Russian troops invaded Poland from the east. Hitler's government ignored the ultimatum.

My grandmother wrote:

I watched the advancement of Germans throughout Europe and I realized that the German occupation in France was also very likely, if not inevitable. I believed that my family had very few viable options left, so we agreed to begin the process of obtaining a visa to get into the United States.

On the morning of September 21, 1939, we woke up early in the morning, ate a light breakfast, and got dressed. It was to be a big day for us. We walked down the spiral staircase of Rusza's walk-up and hopped on the trolley that would take us within moments of the immigration office in the heart of Paris.

We approached the crowded immigration office, where hundreds of others waited for papers to flee France. The office was packed with people pressed together like sardines in a smelly tin. The body odor was overwhelming. Some had even spent days waiting in line to get the documented clearance to leave France.

Although it was packed with people, the room was fairly quiet, except for the sighs of impatience. At the counter all the details of the dialogue between the officials and the citizens could be heard by others waiting. The officials all seemed to have loud and abrasive voices and with heavy French accents, they struggled to speak English. On that chilly September day, many of those waiting had tossed their jackets over their arms, and in accordance with proper etiquette, the men removed their hats.

After an hour, Eva who was nine at the time, asked for a drink. I walked her over to the water fountain in the corner of the room. The high jet of water surprised the young Eva, and it wet her entire face. Both of us giggled at the mishap.

We returned to our seats and I looked down at the number in my hand. There were more than thirty people in front of us, all of whom must have gotten up way before the crack of dawn.

"Klein," yelled out a middle-aged man with a mustache. All three of us marched up to the counter. I fluffed my hair for the occasion.

My husband and child did not speak a word of English, and I was happy to have taken some evening English classes in Vienna. They both stood at the counter staring blankly at the uniformed official.

"What can I do for you?" the official asked abruptly.

"We, all three of us, would like a visa into the United States."

The official glanced at our papers and began shaking his head.

"Where's your identification?" he asked me.

"I don't have any. It was taken from me in Austria during a raid. They never had the audacity, those bastards, to return it, but I just handed you those from my husband and daughter."

The official, still with his head hanging down, lifted his eyes to me with a suspicious expression.

"And how do you expect to get out of the country without the proper identification? What do you think I am — a magician?"

"I don't know," I said. "But you better figure something out."

"Madame, there are many people waiting here, and they all have their papers. What is it that you think I can do for you?"

"Get me out of France!" I insisted, my voice rising an octave.

"Sorry. I need your identification," he said, smashing his stamp on some form.

"I want you to issue me a visa into the United States. I have no way of securing identification. My husband and daughter have theirs," I repeated even louder, so everyone in the room could hear. All the heads turned toward me and I repeated, "Do you hear me? We will not stay in France. They hate us here. We need to get out of this country." I repeated those words over and over.

It seemed as if the officials tried everything to get Regina to step away from the counter, but she was tenacious. Time lagged, and finally a few officials huddled in the corner behind the counter, trying to decide how to tame this lion that had marched into their office.

My grandmother continued:

Finally, one man broke away from the huddle, the vice counsel of the United States in Paris, Taylor W. Gannett. He approached the counter in front of me, pulled his shoulders back, adjusted the glasses on his nose, and said: "In lieu of passports, we shall accept a signed affidavit of your origins." He stared hard at my paper and stood behind the counter with his hands positioned on his hips.

The officer looked deep into my husband's eyes and said: "Your wife just got you and your daughter a visa into the United States. Don't you want to kiss her?"

My husband shrugged his shoulders, turned away, and said: "No." But on our way out the door he stopped and planted a kiss on my cheek.

REPUBLIC OF FRANCE
CITY OF PARIS
EMBASSY OF THE UNITED STATES
OF AMERICA

SS.

AFFIDAVIT IN LIEU OF PASSPORT

I, the undersigned, being duly sworn, depose and say:

That my name is Samuel KLEIN, and that I was born on August 30, 1896, at Tarnow, Poland;

That my wife, Regina Klein, was born on June 22, 1903, at Kalusch, Poland; and that my minor child, Evy Klein, was born on August 12, 1930, at Vienna, Germany;

That my wife and my minor child are accompanying me to the United States;

That I was bearer of FREMDENPASS issued by Po... at Vienna, which expired; and that I am unable to obtain a travel document valid for travel to the United States from the authorities of the country of my birth or French authorities;

That I am executing this affidavit in lieu of passport to enable me and my family to enter the United States.

Samuel Klein

Subscribed and sworn to before me this 21st day of September 1939.

Taylor Gannett
Taylor W. Gannett
Vice Consul of the United
States of America

Personal Description

Height: 6 feet
Hair: grey
Eyes: brown
Marks: none

Immigration affidavit

Reading this section about my grandparents in Europe made me think of when I was seventeen and my grandfather took me on my first trip to Paris. It was there that he taught me the fine art of people-watching, which without me knowing it, inspired the young writer in me. It was also the first time I met his sister, Rusza, and her husband, Schrulek. They were not what I expected. My grandfather painted a larger-than-life image of Rusza. As his eldest sister, his adoration of her ran deep. Because neither Rusza nor her husband drove and couldn't meet us at the airport, we hopped in a taxi, and in his broken French with a German accent, my grandfather gave the driver Rusza's address.

She lived in District VII, which at the time was predominantly a food district. The streets were jammed with people holding bags of groceries in each hand. Each store had a display of food on wooden stands outside, surrounded by shoppers looking for the best deal. I rolled down my window and smelled the horrific fish odor permeating the street.

The taxi driver finally pulled up to what looked like two warehouse doors in the middle of this district. My grandfather noticed my quizzical expression and told me that's where his sister lived.

We pulled out our suitcases from the taxi's trunk and rang the doorbell on the right side of the wooden doors. Within moments a rather short lady with a limp, jovial smile, big cheeks, and pudgy lips, almost looking like a caricature, let us in.

"*Bonjour,* Diana," she said to me. She cupped my chin in her wrinkled hands and said something to my grandfather, which he translated as, "She is pretty."

"*Entrez. Entrez,*" she said motioning us inside. My grandfather put down his bag and gave his sister a big hug and said something in German, the only other language I heard my parents speak at home when they didn't want me to understand something.

Inside those large double doors was a huge courtyard with other doors and signs on the courtyard's perimeter. It was obviously an industrial area. We followed Rusza to a stairwell at the far end leading to her apartment. I later learned that the courtyard was for those working in the textile industry.

We walked up to her second floor apartment, and Schrulek, her rather short and chubby cross-eyed husband, sat reading a newspaper in the living room. When he saw us, he stood up and came to give us a hug. He also had an effervescent smile.

"Would you like something to drink?" my grandfather translated from German. It always seemed as if adults were trying to feed me or offer me drinks. We spent about three days in their tiny apartment with a sewing machine and water heater jammed into the corner of the kitchen. Rusza prepared some wonderful traditional meals that I enjoyed. I recall how she hardly sat down with us; she was busy running back and forth from the stove to the table.

Our big outing during that visit was to her favorite fish restaurant around the corner. It was famously called Flo's. My grandfather was also obsessed with fresh seafood, and this place had plenty of it. It was here where I enjoyed my first piece of salmon. One thing that really surprised me about the restaurant was how everyone brought their dogs to dinner! Underneath nearly every table was a furry creature sitting at the end of some rhinestone leash. This was a huge culture shock for the American girl, where dogs were neither wanted nor allowed in restaurants.

PART THREE

CHAPTER 13

Early Days in New York

In 1939 after arriving in the United States, my grandparents settled in Brooklyn, New York. After a short time they opened a general merchandise store and called it Klein's On Broadway. It was located just around the corner from their brownstone walk-up in the East New York section of Brooklyn. They purchased the store using the letters of credit that Herman wrote for them back in Vienna before World War II.

For my grandparents, the language barrier was a definite impediment in their new country, and like many other immigrants, they struggled. My grandmother had already studied English in Austria. My grandfather, however, only learned English after arriving in the United States by watching the morning and evening news and by reading all the city's newspapers. Within a short period of time, he was able to converse with slow-speaking customers.

By the mid-1950s my grandparents had saved up enough money to buy a small three-bedroom house in a quiet residential part of Fresh Meadows in the borough of Queens in New York.

Each morning, my grandfather, standing tall at six feet with thick hair as white as snow, walked down the hill to Jewel Avenue to catch a bus and a train taking him within steps of his store. His walk was graceful, like I'm sure it was when he met my grandmother at modeling school in Vienna back in the 1920s. He cherished the one-hour train ride, during which time he read the *New York Times* that he folded into quarters so as to not disturb the person seated beside him.

In front of Klein's, located at 1673 Broadway, was the elevated train that brought him to work each day. It was suspended over the street and perhaps contributed to my grandfather's insidious hearing loss. The sound hurt so

Regina's citizenship certificate

badly, you had to cover your ears as it came to a screeching halt.

Finally, when the train stopped, the doors slowly opened and piles of people made their way out, many carrying stuffed shopping bags in both hands as they ran down the steep steel stairway bringing them to the littered street below. Their bags were not always filled with newly purchased items. Sometimes it was just a change of clothes for their work day and a bagged lunch. Many immigrants lived in that section of Brooklyn, and their days were often long. They worked and lived side by side with other immigrants, Afro-Americans (or blacks, as we called them back then), and Puerto Ricans. The homogenous community had a strong flavor back then of hard-working laborers raising their young families.

Klein's catered to this working class of immigrants. The store sold absolutely everything, from Corning Ware to BVD underwear. It was situated on a busy street, nestled between a large Woolworth's and a small butcher shop that hung huge racks of meat in the window. This revolted and fascinated me. When walking down the street, I pretended that I couldn't stand looking at the meat, yet my eyes rolled all the way to the right, sneaking a quick glimpse. Hanging from gigantic hooks, the meat was marbled, flat, and about two feet long, and was swarming with flies. When the butcher went to change the sale sign in the window, he nudged the meat, causing it to sway back and forth like laundry just hung out to dry on a clothesline.

After arriving in the United States, my grandmother's journal no longer discussed either her father or sister. I was surprised to find amongst her papers a telegram received from her brother, Willy, in Israel about their father's death in 1947.

While still spending most of his time managing the store, my grandfather continued to nurture some of his cherished European traditions, such as reading his newspaper on park benches and taking long afternoon coffee breaks. My grandmother often complained about having to work so hard while he leisurely spent time lingering in coffeehouses reading his newspapers. My mother told me that my grandmother was bothered by his behavior. She always made sure there was enough money in the bank, and she was also the one who decided how and where to spend what little earnings they had. She handed over only a small allocation of funds to my grandfather, because if he had more than necessary, he wound up squandering it away.

My grandfather's compulsive gambling habits necessitated frequent trips to Atlantic City. Because he didn't

Regina's father's death, 1947

drive, a few times each year he took the Greyhound bus at the Port Authority Bus Terminal in New York City, which dropped him on the steps of the casinos. Those trips disappointed my grandmother. My grandparents' differing attitudes about what to do with their savings placed a huge strain on their already unstable relationship. Many of their arguments revolved around finances.

To help cope with the strains of her marriage, Regina frequented some of New York City's finest dance halls. Because parking in the city was difficult, she often took a bus and a train from Queens. One winter evening in 1951, when my mother was twenty-one years old, she offered to drive my grandmother to the city. That was an evening she'll never forget.

After arriving at the dance hall, she decided to hang around until my grandmother finished dancing. So she would not be noticed, she chose a quiet table among the row of tables in the rear of the hall. Smiling servers dressed in black and white circulated with trays asking if anyone wanted a drink. The dim lighting was conducive to close dancing and the formation of new relationships.

On this particular evening, the dance hall was almost at capacity and everyone was more dressed up than usual. There was more glitter than on an ordinary evening because it was the dance hall's tenth-anniversary celebration, and complimentary drinks were being offered. My mother sat herself down at a table and my grandmother went off dancing with her regular partner, a man about her age. After a few moments, my mother spotted in the distance a suave gentleman, about ten years her senior. He was dancing with another woman, but each time he spun his partner around, he intentionally made eye contact with my mother. That man was Edward Marquise, a thirty-year-old immigrant who would one day be my father.

Edward had arrived from Germany only four years earlier. He and his older brother, Bob, were the only two survivors from their entire family to survive the horrors of the Holocaust. They spent five years of their adolescence in Dachau's concentration camp. My father never spoke of his experiences in Dachau except to say that he was one of the lucky ones to work in the kitchen peeling potatoes, because one Nazi commander knew his father, who had owned a lumberyard in town. My father could never stand the sight of red meat because he said it reminded him of all the dead corpses seen during his five long years in the concentration camp.

My mother recounted the story of the first time she met my father. He had just finished the dance with his partner and motioned with his fingers for my mother to have the next dance with him. She looked down at her dress and shoes and realized her inappropriate attire. She wore pedal pushers and a floral top with some spots from gardening that morning. She wore flat shoes with leather soles. She had not planned on staying; she was just going to drop her mother off, but Regina invited her in.

Edward sensed that Eva was self-conscious about her looks and motioned that it was okay. Without taking his eyes off her, he meandered in her direction, and with a broad smile exposing his perfectly aligned white teeth, he extended his hand toward her, signaling again to have the next dance. She stood up.

"Thank you, but really I'm not dressed for this. I was just dropping my mother off and she asked me to stay."

"That's okay. You are beautiful. Look at those eyes. Say no more."

He put his arm around her and pulled her onto the dance floor and slipped right into the next dance. At the end of the dance, he walked her back to my grand-mother's table.

"Thank you," she said.

"No, it's me who says thank you. The pleasure was mine," he said, gently taking Eva's hand to plant a kiss.

"Will you have a drink with us?" my grandmother inquired.

"Surely, if that's okay with your daughter."

"Yes, yes," Eva said.

My grandmother took an immediate liking to my father. On their drive home that evening, she told Eva that he would make the perfect husband.

"He has the looks, sense of humor, charm, and manners. You don't always see that in one package," she said. "I am so happy you gave him your telephone number. That was a great idea. He will be good for you, Eva."

"You think so, Mom?"

"Yes. You need not look anymore. You are twenty-one now, and I don't know how long I will be around to look after you. He's the type of man who'll take such good care of you."

My grandmother made frequent references to dying and I think this was tied to her tendency toward depression and possibly her contemplation of suicide. Perhaps this was her way of preparing everyone for the eventuality.

My parents ended up dating for two years before they married on December 27, 1952. My grandmother wanted to be an integral part of their relationship, and they actually enjoyed having her along on their dates. She was a fun-loving and vivacious woman.

After their honeymoon in Daytona Beach, Florida, the newlyweds returned home, and my grandparents offered them an opportunity to move in with them. My mother

*Regina and
Edward*

*Eva and Edward,
1952*

said that Regina made her feel guilty about leaving her alone with Sam, who was rarely home and with whom she had frequent arguments. Days would sometimes pass without them uttering one word to one another. My father welcomed the opportunity to have surrogate parents, especially since losing his own in the Holocaust. Regina and my father had a mutually adoring relationship. Sam, however, never approved of my father, although Edward tried so hard to please Sam by being the obliging son-in-law and always being available to help. Sam didn't believe my father was good enough or educated enough for his only daughter. What he neglected to realize was that as a result of World War II and having been in Dachau for five years, my father was never given the opportunity to attend university.

Over the course of the next two years, the four of them lived in harmony and worked hard at Klein's On Broadway, until everyone's life changed on Mother's Day, 1954.

CHAPTER 14

Regina's Only Grandchild

I was born on May 7, 1954, in the Deaconess Hospital in Brooklyn. The hospital was located around the corner from my grandfather's store. At birth I weighed a meager five pounds. My parents told me that I looked like a monkey, but was the size of chicken. One aunt was angry about their comment and said that the ugliest babies often turned out to be the most beautiful adults!

My mother never wanted to breast-feed me. To her, the idea of nursing was equated with the lower class, and this repulsed her, so I was immediately given the bottle. Later on I learned that my mother never truly enjoyed feeding me, and it was often my grandmother's responsibility. Thankfully, she delighted in the pleasures of nurturing her first grandchild.

My new bedroom was situated on the top of the stairs, securely located between my parents' and my grandparents' room. After I was born, the internal and external landscape of our house completely changed. My father was so excited about my birth that he painted both his Chevrolet and the shingles on our house pink. He also planted a cherry blossom tree on the front lawn. Each year on my birthday, the tree exploded with beautiful pink flowers that after a week or so left a thick pink carpet on the grass. I used to love sitting among the flowers and tossing them up into the air. On each of my childhood birthdays, a picture of me was taken under that tree. My grandmother's bedroom was above the tree, which was barren the day she died.

My grandparents lived with us in that small two-story brick home in Queens, the same one where my mother brought her boyfriends from high school on the weekends. For me, there was a sense of comfort having my grandparents there, a gentle reminder of the passage of time. Our house sat on a street of row houses, each house different and sitting in the center of a quarter of an acre. Even though a fence and established trees separated the properties, we could still see the neighbors' homes. Our backyard featured a manicured lawn with a perimeter of flower gardens and tomato and cucumber plants. My mother was an avid gardener. She also fervently believed in composting, because she said it enriched the soil for the vegetables. A yellow strainer sat in the corner of our kitchen counter holding all the disposables, such as cucumber peelings, wilted lettuce, and cherry pits, which would be brought out to the yard near the fence in the left back corner of the property.

My grandfather often acted awkward with me, not knowing what to say or ask, sort of hemming and hawing with questions, but I knew that he loved me. After all, I was his only grandchild. He had this way of looking at me and speaking to me that made me feel extraordinary

Regina and Samuel, 1954

inside. Perhaps it was the sparkle in his eyes or the softness of his voice. I noticed he didn't smile for anyone else. He acted grumpy when speaking to my parents and grandmother.

Every so often, when my mother wasn't looking, he would slip a twenty-dollar bill into my hand and say, "Buy yourself something," and then plant a kiss on my lips. He then walked away as if he'd get punished for interacting with me.

On a typical day, my grandfather arrived at his store at about eight o'clock in the morning. He'd unlock and lift up the metal gate protecting the store. With another key he unlocked the glass doors. In the still dark store, he approached the light switch in the middle of the store and then hung his coat on the hook in the coffee room in the back. While walking to the back of the store, he swung his head left and right, searching for any mishaps that might have occurred during the evening hours. He then approached the cash register near the front of the store and looked around him and beneath the counter to make sure nobody was hiding before he put the petty cash into the drawer. At the same time, he kept his eyes on the front door to ensure nobody was standing there waiting to hold him up, at which point he would grab the bat he had sitting underneath the cash register. Thankfully he never had to use it.

At nine o'clock at least one customer stood outside waiting for the doors to open. He glanced at his watch and approached the door to let the customer in, usually muttering "Good morning" without looking in their eyes or smiling as he glanced down to make sure that they were not carrying any shopping bags that could be used to steal merchandise from his store. He was not shy about asking customers to leave their bags with him until they finished shopping.

After letting the customers inside, he had this ritual of following them throughout the store with his hands firmly clasped behind his back. Once in a while he asked if he could help them, but he believed that everyone in Brooklyn wanted to steal from him. Sometimes he trailed the customers so closely that he could touch the back of their shoes with his, causing their feet to lift out.

When they first opened the store, my grandmother was the only person working with my grandfather and he was not the easiest person to work with. Until the day I was born, my grandmother worked twelve-hour days each day. When I came along, she opted to stay home and take care of me while my mother worked as a part-time medical receptionist. She then began working only on weekends. My grandmother's radiant spirit cast a different light on the mood at Klein's. The customers liked her, and when she wasn't there, they asked of her whereabouts. She warmly asked them if they were looking for anything in particular, but if they just wanted to look around, that was fine with her. Unlike my grandfather, she never assumed the customers wanted to steal.

Thanks to her positive attitude and intuitive business acumen, Klein's became a neighborhood success story and a place where the locals flocked when looking for variety at good prices. One by one my grandmother sat down with buyers in the employee room in the rear of the store, closed off by a green curtain, to decide what to sell and how to display the store's inventory. She set up two different bank accounts — one personal and one business. Faithfully, at the end of each workday, she walked up the street to the bank clutching a zippered canvas envelope under her arm. It held each day's daily deposits.

My grandmother was a miser and quite talented at handling money. She managed all the bank accounts because when they arrived from Europe, she already spoke English and could more easily deal with the banks. Dettner, the name I somehow invented for my grandmother, had an effervescent spirit and a broad smile that exposed the space between her two front teeth. She had dark brown hair with brown eyebrows that framed her dark eyes, her most striking feature. How they pierced through you! Her high cheekbones were usually highlighted with a dab of rouge.

I loved the way my grandmother looked at me. She had a sublime glow and adoration in her eyes. To gain height next to my six-foot grandfather, she wore very high-heeled shoes, even while working at the store. She must have had every color shoe with a matching purse for

Regina, 1954

each outfit hanging in her walk-in closet, the same closet where all those years her journal had been tucked away.

I got a thrill out of going into her room next to mine. I especially liked wandering into that walk-in closet and snooping around. Sometimes I sat on the floor, and other times I sat on the needlepoint stool that she stood on to reach her important documents in boxes on the top shelf. She was only four feet nine inches tall, so she really needed that stool. The closet had a high ceiling where a string was attached to a single bulb in the center. Pulling the string would turn on the 100-watt bulb.

My grandmother's closet was packed with clothes and shoes. The clothing rack covered three walls of the closet. On one side hung dresses, the other side, skirts and blouses, and on the third side, hung coats and jackets. Her shoes were lined up near the floor on a slanted shoe rack built by my father. In one corner of the closet she had a row of vertical shelves stacked with her matching purses.

One of my favorite things to do was to pull down a purse from those shelves, open it up, and then stick my nose into it. Each purse smelled exactly like her. I wondered if she sprayed Evening in Paris inside so that no one else could use the purse. I let my nose linger usually until I heard someone coming, and then I dashed over to the typewriter on her vanity and pretended to be typing a letter. Each purse also had an embroidered handkerchief tucked inside, and sometimes a stick of red lipstick. Once I took out her lipstick and smeared it all over my lips. That night my mother was so mad when I came down to dinner that she banned me from using the phone for a week.

I was proud of my grandmother's appearance, of her radiance and her elegant strut. She never left the house without being fashionably dressed.

"You never know who you will meet," she told me once when I was about nine years old, "Even if you're just putting the garbage out."

"Why are you all dressed up, Mom?" my eighteen-year-old son used to ask.

"I'm not, I am just dressed," I'd say, hearing my grandmother's voice echo in my head. My grandmother may have also been the reason why I never felt comfortable slipping into a pair of blue jeans unless going for a walk or tinkering in the garden.

My grandmother was probably the best-dressed escort for miles around. My friends frequently commented on her beauty. Once for show-and-tell I brought a photograph to school of my grandmother standing on our inclined driveway wearing a fur coat, her head lifted proudly to the sky. She looked like the model she was in Europe when she met my grandfather at modeling school. My friends weren't surprised when I told them she'd won numerous beauty contests in her native Austria.

For my grandmother, my birth was a gentle reminder of the slippage of time. Soon after I was born, she began reflecting on her frustrations about not finishing medical school. One morning while everyone else was asleep, she sat down at her Remington typewriter and composed a letter to the director of New York University's medical school requesting admission into their program. Back then it wasn't easy for women to pursue professions such as medicine. It was a male-dominated profession. To her greatest disappointment, she was declined admission.

New York, September 1, 1954.

Long Island University
Medical College,
N.Y.

             Gentlemen,

                    Upon graduation from high school
in Vienna, in 1923, I was a student at the faculty of medicine
at the University of Vienna for 2 years from 1923 to 1925.
Though I tried repeatedly I could not obtain a record of
attendance from Vienna.
                    I am now 51 years old; I came here after
the occupation of Vienna in 1939. All those years I worked much
and raised a family. It has been my lifelong, my most cherished
dream to be yet in a position to finish my studies in medicine.
If you would only admit me I would show earnestness of purpose
and would apply myself in my studies to the utmost of my
abilities. I would show myself worth of being admitted to your
College, if you would only find me worth having.

                          Yours respectfully
                          Mrs.Regina Klein
                          7oo9 173 Str.Flushing
                          65--N.Y.

Regina's letter to medical school, 1954

Regina, Samuel, and Diana

CHAPTER 15

Relationships Evolve

In 1960, about the time I entered kindergarten, my mother decided to venture back to full-time work. She was hired as a medical assistant in Dr. Schuster's office on Long Island. Dr. Schuster was a gray-haired and compassionate internist married to a woman who my mother used to call "the witch." Once when I was visiting my mother, I remember his wife storming into the office and yelling as he took her by the hand and escorted her back into the house. He made us believe that she "wasn't all there." I don't remember him being embarrassed about her outbursts. I just remember him being very patient and loving. In many ways, Dr. Schuster was a father image for my mother. She used to talk to him about her problems because she didn't have a good relationship with either her own father or her husband.

My mother said that she returned to work because it was impossible for two women to be in the house at the same time. "I wanted to give your grandmother a reason to wake up in the morning, and taking care of you gave her that."

On the weekends, my grandmother continued to work at Klein's, and she often brought me with her. To-gether we stood behind the cash register collecting money with those old-fashioned cash registers. We had to count the change, and I stood beside her watching her every move. My grandmother had me dressed in frilly girly dresses with matching bows in my hair. Sometimes the bows were almost as large as my head.

At the age of eight, I rang up my first item on the cash register, a stainless steel pan that weighed a ton when I lifted it into the brown paper bag. Standing on my tip-toes, my grandmother told me what numbers to punch in. The register door flung open and nearly knocked me off my stool. I giggled. In front of me stood a lady in her Sunday best, probably returning from church. She reached over the counter and tried to grab me so I wouldn't fall backward.

The next customer in line was an oversized woman with three kids barely reaching her waist. On the counter, she dumped a basket of BVD underwear and socks, from the sale bin my grandfather had set up in the back of the store. My grandmother whispered in my ear to ring each item separately, and she showed me how to give change by counting forward from the sale amount to the number on the paper bill handed to me. She made me feel proud for helping and thanked the customers for their patience. When there was no one left in line, she looked at me, ex-posing the space between her two front teeth, and ex-ploded into a big smile.

"Good work, honey. Grandma is proud of you," she said, hugging me.

At the end of the day we hand counted the earnings.

I remember the anticipation as my grandparents compared the day's numbers to the previous day's. My grandparents tried hard to work together peacefully. Often they would accomplish this by keeping their distance from one another in the store. Entire days passed without them uttering a single word to one another. I remember standing by the front door with my grandmother and her yelling at my grandfather, "We're going for lunch at Woolworth's," and then we'd walk outside to the street with the noisy and smelly train above.

Lunchtime was my favorite time of day. We arrived at the doors of Woolworth's, and I ran quickly into the pie wedge cubicle of the revolving door as my grandmother tried jamming into the same one with me. I then rushed to the counter with swinging barstools overlooking the side street of brownstone walk-ups. I hopped up on the light blue vinyl stools and spun around a few times before ordering my vanilla milk shake and extra-long hot dog with ketchup. After gobbling down my lunch, my grandmother allowed me to wander around the store.

"You have five minutes," she'd tell me, pointing to her almost microscopic gold watch that she held at arm's length to see. At the end of five minutes, I heard her whistle, signaling it was time to return to work.

"Dettner, look at this," I said, holding up a skinny doll with chocolate-colored skin. "It's small enough to fit into my bag, not like Tiny Tears." I was rarely forthright about wanting something, but I thought just mentioning a feature of the doll would lead my grandmother to buy it for me.

"Cute, isn't she? Don't you have one just like that at home?" she asked.

"Not really. You're thinking of Jane. Her legs fell off a long time ago. She is not good anymore, Dettner."

I looked up at her in the hope that she'd buy it for me.

"Let's think about it, honey. Maybe when we come back tomorrow it'll still be here. You're coming to work with Grandma tomorrow, aren't you?"

"It's the last one, Dettner. The others have darker faces and different clothes. She's special," I said, planting a kiss on the doll's forehead.

"You really like that one, don't you, honey?"

"I do."

"All right," she said. "But I don't want to go through this again tomorrow, you hear?"

"Promise," I said, giving her a big wet kiss on the cheek, as I walked out clutching the doll to my chest while my grandmother went to pay.

As time went on, I became independent and needed my grandmother's caretaking less. One day in third grade, I asked permission to walk alone to school, which was only three blocks away. It wasn't that I didn't love my grandmother anymore, but I didn't want my friends to see me with her. Everyone else either biked or walked to school by themselves. In addition to our growing distance, her relationship with my grandfather began deteriorating even further. They bickered more frequently, usually about money. In those days, divorce was considered highly taboo, but my grandparents had a certain resolve about their relationship. My grandfather found ways to keep his distance from grandma. He either worked long hours or took trips to visit his sister, Rusza, in France.

I rarely saw my grandparents speaking to one another, and when they did, they were usually yelling. Very often they would use me to relay messages from one to the other. I just thought this was a cool way to communi-

Regina, age 57

cate and a normal way of doing things after all those years of marriage. I felt special to be the one to relay messages. At the age of nine, I didn't undersatnd the complexity of their relationship or, for that matter, any relationship.

My grandparents slept in the same room, but on twin beds pushed together. Usually one was asleep when the other one entered the room at night, so communication was curtailed. Sometimes they couldn't contain their anger toward one another. I remember once when I was about nine years old, I came downstairs for dinner and saw them both standing on either side of our small living room. They were in the middle of an argument. In her hand, my grandmother held an empty green glass and was getting ready to throw it at my grandfather. When she saw me, she lowered it to her side and they both retreated to the kitchen as if they were going to have breakfast together. I sensed danger and ran back upstairs.

CHAPTER 16

Seeking Restitution

In the early 1960s and before her death in 1964, my grandmother began investigating the possibility of seeking restitution and compensation from European authorities for damages she incurred during her final years in Vienna, which was ultimately the beginning of World War II. These letters were originally written in German and have been translated.

One of my grandmother's first letters was written to the director of the Compensation Office in Trier, Germany. Here is that letter:

August 6, 1960

Dear Director:

As you can see by the enclosed documents, I have sought damages for the past three years with the United Restitution Office in New York. What was communicated to me was that the petition must be sent to you.

I have accumulated endless papers like this — the papers could have almost spanned the largest ocean. It is already twenty-two years since the occupation of Austria. I am therefore long overdue for the payment of my damages if I am ever to receive them in my lifetime.

I am already fifty-seven years old, in poor health, and it is about time I get some help. I believe, Mr. Director, that you will agree with me. That is why I would like you to give me your full attention concerning my application. I implore you to provide me with a favorable outcome.

Otherwise, how will your help be useful when I am no longer alive? I left Vienna with my eight-year-old child Eva, and I now have a granddaughter of that same age. The memories of my past are so terrible that I believe I deserve a reward for my damages. I need this reward soon. Hopefully your help does not arrive too late.

I thank you in advance for your effort. I ask your forgiveness if you find this letter sounding somewhat bitter.

> *Respectfully,*
> *Regina Klein*

After reading this letter I wondered if my grandmother had already begun contemplating suicide. She made two references to suicide and it possibly being too late to receive any sort of restitution. In subsequent letters, she suggested that the authorities move quickly on her case, saying such things as, "How long is a person's total life?" and "How long do you think I will live?" It is unclear whether this was her strategy to rush the authorities along or if she had already begun contemplating suicide.

My understanding was that she never received any

response from the Restitution (Compensation) Office in Germany, so she decided to hire Dr. Evian, an attorney in Vienna. This is her first correspondence to him:

May 28, 1962

Dear Doctor:

I would like to pass over my claim for restitution to you, made in Trier, Germany. The file number is 253–188, Department B. It has been outstanding for years.

I have made my claim to Vienna and was then referred to Trier from Austria. In September 1957 I made a claim through the United Restitution Organization in New York for damages to my health and deprivation of my freedom. The only success I have had up until now is that I received $100 U.S. for the deprivation of freedom.

My name is Regina Reinharz Klein, born June 22, 1903 in Poland. I have lived in Vienna since 1916. In 1927 I married a Polish citizen, Samuel Klein. In 1930 I had a child, Eva, born in Vienna.

On November 12, 1938, my apartment in Vienna was overtaken in a raid. During this occurrence I was overtaken with force, suffered bleeding from my kidneys, and endured severe kidney damage, which resulted in my needing an operation. I am still plagued with pain and inconveniences, nearly twenty-five years later. I have all the accumulated piles of papers. Please inform me under what conditions you will take on my case and which papers you will need from me.

Regina Klein
Flushing 65, NY

Dr. Evian wrote back that he would be delighted to take on her case. He notified her that there would be a 10 percent fee of the total sum of the awarded damages. After signing the attorney's affidavit, she wrote a nasty letter to the United Restitution Organization. She told them how impatient she was with their response to her request. She said that as a result of their slow reply, she was forced to hire an attorney. "If things continue in this fashion, I'll have to live a hundred years in order to get any sort of resolution," she wrote.

Here is an excerpt from a subsequent letter written to Dr. Evian:

What do I know? I am helpless because a kidney was taken from me and I suffer daily because of it. I have nephrosis, and had a difficult operation and nothing to show for it. I am giving you a copy of my letter and copies of all the doctor's statements, which I have already sent to the USO office in Trier. I don't need them and won't be taking them to my grave.

This emphatic letter illustrates my grandmother's impatience to resolve this claim and her sense that her life was coming to an end. In the same letter, she mentioned that her husband's annual income in Vienna was between twelve and fourteen schillings. She confessed that she was arrested while in her apartment and was thrown against the fireplace and beaten up. As a result of this incident, she suffered kidney damage and was then operated on in the Politiklinik by Dr. Fritch. Her final diagnosis was hydronephrosis.

Here is another letter written by an employee from my grandparent's store in Vienna. It was also addressed to the United Restitution Organization in New York. It seems to be a letter of reference indicating my grand-mother was in good standing in Austria.

November 13, 1961

Dear Sirs:

Regina Klein (maiden name Reinharz) and I went to school together. We both lived before the persecution in Vienna, where her husband, Samuel, owned a men's cloth-ing store. Furthermore, I confirm that the above-mentioned couple lived in a six-room apartment in Vienna for three years as good citizens. The business mentioned above belonged to Regina's brother, and Regina's husband worked for him. I was visiting Regina when the SS officers, in November 1938, arrested her, hit her, and took her away during a raid. Her daughter, Eva, was also there and was taken away with her mother. Finally, I also confirm that the above-mentioned per-son was a healthy person before the mentioned events, but was very sick when she returned after three months from the ar-rest. She told me at that time that she was treated poorly. I have not filed for compensation with the German authori-ties. Since that time, I fled to England and lived in London un-til I immigrated to the United States on the Queen Elizabeth in 1948.

Clara Breir

CHAPTER 17

Final Days

The most shocking documents I found in my grandmother's closet were her requests for separation from my
grandfather. My grandmother had filed for separation on
grounds that my grandfather had physically abused her
while working at Klein's. When I asked my mother, she
said that my grandparents were legally separated but continued to live under the same roof. As a child I wasn't
privy to any of this. I saw them as married but acting rude
to one another. I assumed that's what happened after
years of marriage.

    I found the entire situation difficult to fathom, par-
ticularly in view of my own memories of my grandfather.
What I recall about him was that he was a quiet man who,
after a long day of work, would sit in the living room,
watching the evening news on his 12-inch television on
the glass coffee table set between the sofas. He minded
his own business. I have no recollection of any aggressive

Mr. H. W. Tannenbaum Esq., attorney for Samuel Klein, was
kind enough to come to our office to discuss with us the terms
for a proposed separation between Samuel and Regina Klein. The
following are the proposed tentative terms. This is what counsel
has agreed to discuss with their respective clients:

1. Support payments $90.00 per week net.   *150.00*

2. Stock in Klein's of Broadway Inc. to be divided equally
between husband and wife, wife to give husband voting proxy.   *No-LE;*

3. Taxpayer on Broadway, Brooklyn, to be conveyed to tenancy
in common. Rent figure for store is left open. Rent to be
negotiated.   *EVA*

4. House at 70-09 173rd Street to be conveyed to ~~Diane~~
Marquise.

5. Counsel fees to be equally divided between counsel, $2750.

1500.00
1460.00
30.
120.00
600.00

Regina and Samuel's separation agreement, 1962

behavior on his part. I do remember him putting on an angry face when my grandmother walked into the room. I remember seeing respect, but not love, in his eyes. If under stress, he would resort to a quiet walk rather than to violent gestures. He might have lifted his hand with the impulse to hit, but I couldn't actually imagine him following through. As children, we don't usually question relationships as much as we do as adults. There were times when I intuitively felt things were not exactly right between my grandparents. I was confused because nobody communicated anything to me. As an adult, I realized it was likely that my grandmother fabricated the story about being hit in order to find her way out of a bad marriage. But from what I remember about her, she was not a dishonest woman.

My grandmother was very possessive of me, and only after she died did my grandfather and I become much closer.

Each Sunday my grandfather took me on a date to New York City. His favorite spot was Stouffer's Restaurant on top of the 666 Building. One trip when I was twelve years old really stands out in my mind. I'd asked him that week if we could do our outing on Friday instead of Sunday. I told him that I had an important paper due on Monday.

"Are you sure you can't go?" he asked, obviously sounding disappointed and cherishing our outings together.

"I'm sure, Grandpa. It's the end of the semester and it's an important assignment. My mother was going to take me to the library to finish my research."

"I have an idea," he said. "How about we go to the library in the city? That'll be an adventure."

"That big one with all the stairs?"

"No, not the main library. It's too busy there. Let's try the one on 55th Street, directly across the street from the Museum of Modern Art."

That museum was one of my grandfather's favorites, particularly because it was just up the street from Stouffers.

"Okay. That's a good idea. Sure. I'll pack my books."

We arrived at the library, and it made me feel mature doing an assignment in a big city library. I remember after introducing me to the librarian, my grandfather sat patiently reading the *New York Times* in the periodical section. After completing my assignment, we went to Stouffer's, where the waitress teased me about being my grandfather's girlfriend.

Once in a while on our outings, my grandfather surprised me with theater tickets for a Broadway show. Our relationship revolved around those weekend outings and around clothing shopping together. I sensed the joy it gave him to help me choose my wardrobe. I also trusted his taste in clothes. He was so savvy about what was in style. Receiving my grandfather's undivided attention was also a vital part of my adolescence. My grandfather became my best friend and grounded me between the inner adolescent angst and the chaotic world surrounding me growing up in New York in the 1960s.

The summer I turned seventeen, he took me to Paris to visit his sister, Rusza. We went on long walks and then we'd sit for hours in the busy cafés. His favorite one was Café de la Paix, where we indulged in our favorite pastime of people-watching.

During every Christmas holiday I visited my grandfather in Miami, where he spent the cold winter months.

He lived with a Cuban family who adored him. In the evenings he took me dancing at the fanciest of Miami's hotels, including the infamous Fontainebleau on Collins Avenue. My grandfather never spoke about my grandmother, and I knew not to ask, because they had such a painful relationship. It was just a sensitive subject.

My grandfather danced at my wedding at the St. Moritz Hotel in New York in 1977. Simon and I married while still in school. He was finishing his Doctorate at McGill University in Montreal, and I had just begun nursing school after receiving a baccalaureate in health administration and journalism.

At the end of May 1980, while studying for my nursing licensure exams, my mother phoned.

"Diana, your grandfather has just come in from his walk around the block. He complained of a really bad stomachache, so he went to his internist, who sent him to the hospital right away. There they diagnosed him with a ruptured aortic aneurysm. I'm so upset, Diana. He needs immediate surgery," she said tearfully, with more emotion than I ever remember my mother having.

I was torn about where to be or what to do. I asked my mother what she thought.

"I think you should stay in Montreal and take your nursing exams. Why don't you visit him next week when he gets home? You'll be more help to me then too."

My grandfather was on the operating room table for more than twelve hours — a lengthy surgery for an eighty-three-year-old man. As a neophyte registered nurse who had already done a rotation in the operating room of a teaching hospital, I was suspicious that they'd used my grandfather for experimental surgery.

Much to my dismay, I never got the chance to kiss my grandfather good-bye. On June 22, 1980 (which coincidentally was my grandmother's birthday), he died of surgical complications.

While he was alive, my grandfather never spoke to me about my grandmother's death. I don't think he wanted to say anything bad in front of me, so he wisely chose not to say anything — at all. In this way I was left with only good memories of my grandmother, and the bitterness between my grandparents never interfered with my relationship with either one of them. I feel lucky to have benefited from two wonderful but completely independent relationships with both my grandparents, and those memories will live with me forever. They gave me an additional perspective on life that contributed to my own confidence and success.

A few years after my grandfather died, I had an interesting encounter with a woman who in so many ways reminded me of my grandmother.

At the time, there was a nurse shortage in the psychiatric unit, so I was asked to leave the cardiac unit and help out in the psychiatric unit. On that day I was given only one "client," as we called them back then. Her name was Mrs. G., because she had a long Polish name that nobody could pronounce.

The day began with morning rounds involving the doctors, nurses, and nursing students going from room to room to visit all the clients on the unit. The head nurse, or physician-in-chief, summarized the reason for the patients' hospitalization and their current status. Sometimes a client's condition evoked a discussion, other times the clan moved rather quickly from one room to the next.

When we entered Mrs. G.'s room, I was at the back of the line. When my eyes set on Mrs. G.'s, I was stunned beyond words. I thought I was looking in the eyes of my grandmother. Her dark hair and well-defined eyebrows matched those of my grandmother. She was applying her lipstick, and her mannerisms reminded me so much of my grandmother's. She used a lip liner to make her lips larger, coming to a well-defined point on the top.

"I just feel naked without my lipstick," my grandmother used to tell me, and I sensed that Mrs. G. echoed similar sentiments.

She had finished applying her lipstick and was sitting up in bed, dressed in a pink skirt and matching floral blouse. This striking sixty-something woman sat up in her bed staring out the window. Her dark eyes emanated intelligence, pain and reflection. I wondered if my grandmother's eyes showed the same pain before she took her own life.

The chief doctor introduced himself to Mrs. G. and asked how she was doing. She muttered something softly, to which the doctor barely responded. We then all convened in the corridor as he continued the discussion.

"Mrs. G. has been depressed for many months. Her family admitted her because she tried to commit suicide by taking an overdose of her blood pressure pills." The mere sound of the word "suicide" made it feel as if a dagger had been plunged deep inside my heart. I was glad to have gulped down a bowl of cereal that morning. It helped ease the nausea caused by this encounter.

One doctor asked the nurse about her medications. Another inquired about the plan for her. After all the questions were answered, the troop of nurses and doctors moved on to the next client. I hung to the back of the group and then stepped inside the room to get a better look at Mrs. G. Unfortunately she had just drifted into a sleep or pretended to do so.

Mrs. G. was oblivious to my presence. I don't know if there were actually sheer curtains swaying near the window, or if my mind put them there, thinking of the last time I saw my grandmother's face.

The head nurse walked toward me and whispered, "Mrs. G. attempted to kill herself the night she found her husband, twenty years her junior, sleeping with another woman."

I gasped.

I couldn't leave the room. I felt a gravitational pull causing me to stay with her. I nudged myself closer to her bed in the small private room with the window overlooking the hospital's roof. I carefully drew the opaque curtains around her bed and sat on the vinyl chair beside. Part of me wanted to wake her in order to hear her voice, her tone, her story. Another part of me was petrified. I stared until hearing the head nurse's footsteps outside the curtain. Her head peeked through the opening.

"Are you okay?" she asked.

I nodded, afraid to admit how the woman resembled my grandmother, both in appearance and mannerisms. I thought about the possibility of them dismissing me from the unit for having a family history of suicide. I wondered if they could even do that. On the other hand, with my background, I felt like I *should* be there.

That evening I pulled out my journal to write about the day's experience. I glanced up at the framed saying hanging above my desk written by Francois Mauriac in his book *The Desert of Love:*

> We are, all of us, molded and remolded by those who have loved us, and though that love may pass, we remain none the less their work — a work that very likely they do not recognize, and which is never exactly what they intended.

After reading my grandmother's documents and having conversations with close relatives, it became evident she had unresolved issues that plagued her life. The memories of her childhood continued to haunt her as she moved forward in life. The stress of not receiving her compensation, coupled with a troubled marriage and my increasing independence, left her with vast feelings of loneliness and hopelessness. As a result of these events, she was tossed deep into the throes of depression. According to my mother, she also had difficulty adjusting to the aging process. It seemed as if she was more afraid of aging than she was of dying, and looking back, I recall one incident from my childhood that resonates with these sentiments.

My grandmother's art deco vanity was pushed against the wall near a window in her bedroom. It was a rather large vanity with three tiers. On the middle tier she stored her makeup and on the tier to the left she had her typewriter, the same one she taught me to type on. I remember walking into her room once (she usually left the door open and didn't mind if I entered) to find her crying in front of the mirror.

"What's wrong, Grandma?" I inquired.

"Oh honey. Never mind. You wouldn't understand."

"How do you know, Grandma? Please tell me."

"I'm getting old, honey. Look at all these wrinkles. I don't like growing old."

"Mom says that we grow old from the day we were born, Grandma."

"That's true, dear. Never mind."

"You are beautiful, Grandma," I said.

"Oh darling, my little *Kinder*," she said pulling me close to her. "What would I do without you? You are so wonderful."

"I love you, Grandma."

"I love you more."

And so we arrived at the spring of 1964 when my parents and I took a vacation to Bermuda. That was the first time we'd taken a holiday without inviting my grandmother. Even though my father adored my grandmother, he thought that year would be a good one for just my parents and me to go away alone. My grandmother didn't seem to have any apparent objections when we left. My parents and I had spent one glorious week, and I can still hear the sounds of the Bermudian men playing percussion during our beachside dinners. The ambiance was elegant and invigorating as the ocean breeze whisked through my long and wavy brown hair. I remember being allowed to wear my beige sleeveless crepe dress, the one I had worn months earlier for the sixth grade dance, the first time I was permitted to shave my legs and wear nylons.

When we returned home from Bermuda, my grandmother met us at the back door, smiling and happy to see us, but there was an underlying sense of sadness and gloom. On the stove she had a big pot of her famous Viennese dish of broad noodles, cottage cheese and raisins. It was my favorite meal that she prepared. We sat down at the light gray Formica kitchen table with the metal rim and black leather swivel chairs. My mother always liked art deco.

My father reminded me to go wash my hands, as he had so many times before. We then all sat down to eat. After we each took our first forkful of food, my grandmother looked at me and asked about our trip. Either she was ignoring my parents or just paying attention to me, I don't remember. Looking back, I know she was upset with them for leaving her behind.

"How was your week?" I asked her.

"Well, it was very quiet here, as you can imagine," my grandmother said. "I don't like this being alone stuff."

My parents looked at one other, and I could tell they didn't know what to say.

"Well, knowing you, we're sure you kept busy," my mother blurted out.

"Never busy enough," my grandmother said.

"I hope you're not mad at us for leaving you behind," my mother asked.

Grandma didn't lift her eyes from her plate, but in her elegant way she maneuvered the noodles in her mouth.

"Mad?" she said." I wouldn't call it mad. Disappointed. Yes. Disappointed."

"I'm sorry you feel that way. We just wanted to have a vacation for the three of us. You know we always invite you. All those years of trips," my mother said.

My father, who was the one who usually spoke, remained silent. It was clear that it was his decision, and three months later, when she took her life, he asked for Regina's forgiveness as he gave her a last kiss on her forehead.

From the moment we returned and for the last few months of my grandmother's life, she didn't laugh as easily and spent increasingly more time alone. She sometimes wandered up our quiet residential street for long solitary walks. My mother said that my grandmother had also begun taking low doses of Valium, and sleeping pills had become a staple in her bedtime routine.

VISION OF RECORDS
ARTMENT OF HEALTH
ROUGH OF QUEENS
FILED

Certificate of Death 156-64-411534

Certificate No.

SEP 8 PM 2:39

1. NAME OF DECEASED *(Print or Typewrite)*

REGINA KLEIN

First Name | Middle Name | Last Name

PERSONAL PARTICULARS
(To be filled in by Funeral Director)

MEDICAL CERTIFICATE OF DEATH
(To be filled in by the Physician)

2. USUAL RESIDENCE: (a) State NEW YORK

(b) Co. QUEENS (c) Town or FLUSHING

(d) No. 70-09-173RD

(e) Length of residence or stay in City of New York immediately prior to death 27/18

3. SINGLE, MARRIED, WIDOWED, (OR DIVORCED) *(write the word)* MARRIED

4. DATE OF BIRTH OF DECEDENT (Month) (Day) (Year)

5. AGE 61 yrs.

6. a Usual Occupation HOUSEWIFE

b Kind of Business or Industry O.A.

7. SOCIAL SECURITY NO. 142-14-6331

8. BIRTHPLACE *(State or Foreign Country)* POLAND

9. OF WHAT COUNTRY WAS DECEASED A CITIZEN AT TIME OF DEATH U.S.A.

10a. WAS DECEASED EVER IN UNITED STATES ARMED FORCES? NO   10b. IF YES, Give war or dates of service

11. NAME OF FATHER OF DECEDENT O.K.

12. MAIDEN NAME OF MOTHER OF DECEDENT O.K.

16. PLACE OF DEATH: (a) NEW YORK CITY: (b) Borough QUEENS

(c) Name of Hospital or Institution QUEENS GENERAL HOSPITAL

(d) If elsewhere than in hospital or institution, give street and number

17. DATE AND HOUR OF DEATH (Month) September (Day) 8 (Year) 1964 (Hour) 10:45 p.

18. SEX Female   19. AGE 60 yrs.

20. I HEREBY CERTIFY that, in accordance with the provisions of law, I took charge of the dead body at Queensboro Mortuary

7th day of September 64

I further certify from the investigation and post mortem examination (with autopsy) that, in my opinion, death occurred on the date and at the hour stated above and resulted from (suicide) and that the causes of death were:

PART I
(a) Immediate Cause POISONING BY BARBITURATES AND OTHER DRUGS; SUICIDE.

(b) and (c) Antecedent Cause with Primary Cause Stated Last

Part II Contributory Causes TENSION PNEUMOTHORAX.

M. E. Case No. 3656   Signed _____ M.D.
(Deputy Chief) Medical Examiner

13. NAME OF INFORMANT EDWARD MAROUSE   RELATIONSHIP TO DECEASED SON-IN-LAW   ADDRESS 70-09-173RD ST FLUSHING N.Y.

14. Place of Cemetery or Crematory BETH DAVID CEMETERY ELMONT L.I.   14a. Location (City, Town or County and State)   14b. Date of Burial or Cremation SEP. 9, 1964

15. FUNERAL DIRECTOR JEFFER FUNERAL HOMES INC   ADDRESS 188-11 Hillside Ave HOLLIS 23 N.Y.

BUREAU OF RECORDS AND STATISTICS   DEPARTMENT OF HEALTH   THE CITY OF NEW YORK

Regina's death certificate, 1964

CHAPTER 18

Lessons from Grandma

In May 2001, after my annual mammogram, I received one of those dreaded phone calls requesting my return to the hospital for some additional views. Alarmed but not terrified, I dragged myself back to the hospital's radiology department, signed my name on the clipboard, took a number, and sat in the waiting room among other anxious women surrounded by tables splattered with outdated magazines. It was the third year in a row that they had called me back for additional mammogram views. Although thankful for the radiologist's attention to my breasts, a part of me felt annoyed by the inconvenience that in previous years ended up being false alarms.

According to my readings and what I had studied in nursing school, I calculated my risk for breast cancer as relatively low. There was no breast cancer in my family — no cancer of any kind. My lifestyle incorporated all the cancer preventatives advocated in national magazines and newspapers. I exercised diligently, never took birth control pills, ingested my daily cocktail of minerals and herbs, stayed away from red meat, munched on soybeans, and drank wine only occasionally. Each of my children was breast-fed, and the literature promised that this factor alone could slip me into a low-risk category. Part of me sat in the waiting room with an air of confidence, yet another part of me feared I might not be as lucky this time around.

I glanced at the innocuous paintings of animals hanging on the wall and at the rushing about of white lab-coated personnel as millions of questions whipped through my mind. I thought of being an only child. What if an unborn sister carried the gene for breast cancer? What about family secrets kept from me? I kept thinking — Why me? Why now? Why here?

That waiting room was the first of many where I would sit during the subsequent year. My breast cancer saga led to disturbed weeks laden with biopsies, blood tests, long waits for results, and a great deal of mental anguish. In the end, it was recommended that I hop on a plane to Los Angeles for a mastectomy and reconstruction under the direction of Dr. Mel Silverstein, a world-renowned specialist in my type of breast cancer (D.C.I.S. or ductal carcinoma in situ).

During those months of anguish, I thought a lot about my grandmother. I reached out to her spirit and her love, which I craved so much during difficult times. Once again I wondered if she had breast cancer but had kept it a secret. I reread her journal over and over again. I searched my mother's archives for old documents of information about my grandmother that might have shed some light on my own predicament, even if it was an old doctor's report. Much to my dismay, nothing was found.

I also thought long and hard about the section of her journal where my grandmother spoke about not feeling loved by her mother. I thought about the first words out of my mother's mouth when I phoned her to tell her about my breast cancer: "Oh no. I better go have my mammogram, I'm late," she said in a voice offering little solace.

I had never thought about my grandmother's depression until I met my own demons with depression after my diagnosis. I had always feared depression more than I feared death. In my twenties and thirties and early forties, I veered away from any discussion about depression. To me it was the poison that killed my grandmother and also infiltrated my mother's life. I never wanted depression to touch my life or my children's. My commitment to that concept dissipated when I was diagnosed with breast cancer. I seemed to have little control over my emotions. At the time, it was difficult to ascertain if my bouts of depression were due to premenopausal issues or my new diagnosis or a combination of them both.

I began reading about depression and its genetic component. I thought about my mother's depression and realized how it began around the time of my grandmother's death. My mother became overwhelmingly sad. She began dressing in black. This drove my father bonkers, because he was a man who adored bright colors like red and yellow. There was some talk of her moods being hormonal, but they also could have been genetically related.

Sometimes when my mother fell into one of her depressive moods, she'd say she couldn't take life anymore. Once I came home from school and she was curled up in a fetal position on her bed. I tried to talk to her and find out what was wrong, but she didn't answer me. "Just leave me alone." I knew I hadn't done anything to hurt her.

"Come on, what's wrong with you? Get up out of bed. Look around you," my father yelled that night, "you've got everything. Look at my life and what I've been through. Do you ever hear me complaining? No. I'm only grateful," he added.

My father never understood why my mother cried so much. Sometimes he asked me if there was a secret she was holding back. Did she have cancer? Was she sick with something terminal? Was she in love with someone else?

My mother didn't always act depressed. Sometimes she was jovial. I was intrigued yet aggravated by my mother's diametric personalities. When she was on the phone with friends, she put on this soft and tender voice, sometimes with a giggly tone, like she was the happiest lady in the world, without a worry. Then she'd hang up, turn around, and return to her long-faced and gloomy demeanor. The contrast was too much for a kid to fathom.

When my mother returned to some semblance of "a normal mood," we never knew when or what brought it on. It seemed random. After my psychiatric residency in Montreal at the age of twenty-two, I began to understand both my grandmother's and my mother's behavior. I learned about the mood swings inherent to the disease.

I learned that often there are no triggers; mood changes just happen. Manic depression is so common — afflicting about 4 million Americans. A few years ago I picked up *An Unquiet Mind: A Memoir of Moods and Madness* by Dr. Kay Redfield Jamison. It provided me with tremendous insight into the disorder. Jamison is a psychiatrist also suffering from manic depressive disease. Being afflicted with the very disease for which she treats her patients provides her with compelling insight. In her book, she works hard helping the reader slip into the psyche of the depressive personality. She sums it up by saying, "My hair like my moods goes up and down." For many years, Jamison took lithium, and said that once she accepted her illness, instead of fighting it, her life became much more bearable.

Books explain how depression can be hereditary. I think some people, and I may be one of those, may be prone to depression as a result of their genetic pool, but external triggers can also spring us into the depressive realm. This is what happened to my grandmother as a result of her turbulent childhood and marriage. This is also what happened to my mother as a result of her unhappy marriage and the loss of her mother, who was the anchor in her life. And for me, it was my diagnosis with breast cancer that landed me in the depression ballpark, a place I had never before visited.

When we look for reasons why a loved one would take his or her life, we rummage through our memories, large and small, poignant and delightful, dramatic and banal, horrible and wonderful, in the search for answers. After arriving at the end of my grandmother's journal, I understand how a slow accumulation of a history filled with hardships and horror could result in sudden actions, seemingly inexplicable yet somehow logical, such as suicide.

Perhaps Labor Day weekend in 1964 marked the end of summer and the beginning of my new school year, or yet another traumatic argument with her distant husband. That year also marked the Beatles coming to America, Jack Ruby being given the death sentence, and South Vietnamese forces initiating the largest attack of the war against Communist guerrillas.

Whatever compelled my grandmother to finally give up, surely it was a result of the culmination of a life spent in hardship. Her life story was one that she felt compelled to share in her retrospective journal. I'm glad that she wrote the journal and even more delighted that she chose to keep it tucked away in her closet, because she could have just as easily destroyed it. Had she done that, I would never have found it, and writing this book would not have been possible.

Writing and studying my grandmother's life has been my way of keeping her alive. Sharing her story has also brought on a compulsion to understand who she was, what she had been through, and why she ended her life. After reading her journal and knowing her for ten years, I realized that there were many aspects of our personalities and sensibilities that were similar. We were both strong and resilient women in the face of disaster, and we were both caretakers. This link remains strong.

The other very important link between us was that we both found solace in journal writing, a ritual that I advocate not only in my own life, but also in my family and in the classroom. When life takes an unexpected turn, I have found that writing becomes my best friend. Journaling is a process of self-discovery and a cathartic way to spill feelings. I have my grandmother to thank for this practice.

I've completed this book only a few years after what would have been my grandmother's one hundredth birthday. As I neared the end of its writing, every image and every memory of her has been recalled, and the result is a renewed understanding of her life and what she endured. The journey has helped me realize that a life without love is no life at all, and that those who have survived severe childhood traumas continue to live with the pain until the day they die. It is with this new understanding that I will hold Regina's soul close to my heart.

∞

Afterword

Herman remained in Vienna with his wife until he died in 1970 at the age of sixty-eight. They never had children. Willy, her eldest brother, moved to Israel in 1916 and worked for the Israeli Postal Service until his death in 1982 at the age of eighty-four. His adopted daughter, Derora, whom I interviewed for this book, had two children and two grandchildren, living in Israel. Derora Reinharz Calderon is a very well-known artist in Israel, and her tapestries appear in many prestigious galleries.

In 1997, I visited Derora and her family in Israel. Derora didn't speak one word of English, which is quite unusual for Israelis. My mother told me that an American soldier had beaten her up, so she decided never to learn the language. So my dear cousin David Nameri, on my father's side, accompanied us to Derora's house in Haifa so that I could ask many questions about her father and my grandmother, her aunt.

Derora said, "Your grandmother had a good relationship with my father, Willy. He always said good words about her. I remember she used to send us many care packages. They were full of beautiful clothes and delicious food. I really looked forward to them. In 1948 we had nothing in Israel. It was wartime and her packages were such a treasure for us. She was a special woman. My father really loved her, and I am only sorry that I never got to meet her."

Beronia, my grandmother's sister, also moved to Israel. She got married and had two children. She and her husband owned a coin shop in Jerusalem. After ten years of marriage, she began having serious bouts of depression. Her husband was very good-looking, and she became increasingly jealous whenever a woman looked his way. Beronia didn't have my grandmother's beauty; she was rather homely. In 1948 their son and daughter were drafted by the Israeli army to fight in the Arab–Israeli War. Within days they were both killed. This event led to Beronia's demise.

The doctors were unable to control her illness with counseling and medications alone, so they admitted her to an institution, where she died in 1990 at the age of eighty-three. She lived in Israel for more than forty years, so says the obituary my cousin David sent from Israel years ago.

My father died in 1991 at the age of seventy from congestive heart failure, a few months short of my parents' fortieth anniversary. My grandmother was right — he loved my mother until the day he died. My mother is still alive and well and living in the home they bought together on Long Island in 1983.

Simon and I have been married thirty years and have three beautiful children, Rachel Miriam (24), Regine Anna (22), and Joshua Samuel (18). We are a very close knit family and I cherish every day we spend together. My diagnosis with breast cancer six years ago became the personal context for writing this story of survival.

BIBLIOGRAPHY

Beller, Steven. *Vienna and the Jews 1867–1938: A Cultural History*. Cambridge: Cambridge University Press, 1989.

Ettinger, Moyshe. "Kalush — Our Native Town: A General View," trans. Adah B. Fogel. In *Kalusz: The Life and Destruction of the Community*, eds. Shabtai Unger and Moyshe Ettinger, 576–563. Tel Aviv, Israel: Kalusz Society, 1980.

Healy, Maureen. *Vienna and the Fall of the Habsburg Empire: Total War and Everyday Life in World War I*. Cambridge: Cambridge University Press, 2004.

Jamison, Kay Redfield. *An Unquiet Mind: A Memoir of Moods and Madness*. New York: Knopf Publishing Group, 1995.

Keegan, John. *The First World War*. New York: Vintage Books, 2000.

Morton, Frederic. *Thunder at Twilight: Vienna 1913/1914*. Cambridge, MA: De Capo Press, 2001.

Pauley, Bruce F. *From Prejudice to Persecution: A History of Austrian Anti-Semitism*. Chapel Hill: University of North Carolina Press, 1992.

Rechter, David. *The Jews of Vienna and the First World War*. London: Littman Library of Jewish Civilization, 2001.

Wachstein, Sonia. *Too Deep Were Our Roots: A Viennese Jewish Memoir of the Years between the Two World Wars*. Sag Harbor, NY: Harbor Electronic Publishing, 2001.

Zweig, Stefan. *The World of Yesterday*. Lincoln: University of Nebraska Press, 1964.